Training and Development Strategy

Andrew Mayo

Andrew Mayo is a consultant in people and organisational development, operating internationally. A BSc in chemical engineering and an MSc in management, he has worked for nearly 30 years in major international organisations, leaving his last post as director of human resource development for the ICL Group in October 1995. He is a Fellow of the IPD and also of the Royal Society of Arts. He is the author of *Managing Careers: Strategies for organisations* (1991), co-author (with Elizabeth Lank) of *The Power of Learning* (1994) and contributor of an essay on economic indicators of HRM to *Strategic Prospects for HRM* (1995, edited by Professor Shaun Tyson), all published by the IPD. He is a frequent speaker at business schools and public seminars.

In the TRAINING ESSENTIALS series leading experts focus on the key issues in contemporary training. The books are thoroughly comprehensive, setting out the theoretical background while also providing practical guidance to meet the 'hands-on' needs of training practitioners. They are essential reading for trainers and for students working towards training qualifications – N/SVQs, and Diploma and Certificate courses in training and development.

Other titles in the series include:

Cultivating Self-Development David Megginson and Vivien Whitaker

Delivering Training Suzy Siddons

Designing Training Alison Hardingham

Developing Learning Materials Jacqui Gough

Evaluating Training Peter Bramley

Facilitation Skills Frances and Roland Bee

Identifying Training Needs Tom Boydell and Malcolm Leary

Introduction to Training Penny Hackett

Psychology for Trainers Alison Hardingham

The Institute of Personnel and Development is the leading publisher of books and reports for personnel and training professionals, students, and all those concerned with the effective management and development of people at work. For full details of all our titles, please contact the Publishing Department:

tel. 020-8263 3387
fax 020-8263 3850
e-mail publish@ipd.co.uk

The catalogue of all IPD titles can be viewed on the IPD website:
www.ipd.co.uk

TRAINING ESSENTIALS

CREATING A TRAINING AND DEVELOPMENT STRATEGY

Andrew Mayo

INSTITUTE OF PERSONNEL AND DEVELOPMENT

First published in 1998
Reprinted 1999

Design and typesetting by Paperweight
Printed in Great Britain by
The Cromwell Press, Wiltshire

British Library Cataloguing in Publication Data
A catalogue record for this book is available from the
British Library

ISBN
0-85292-732-0

INSTITUTE OF PERSONNEL
AND DEVELOPMENT

IPD House, Camp Road, London SW19 4UX
Tel.: 020 8971 9000   Fax: 020 8263 3333
Registered office as above. Registered Charity No. 1038333.
A company limited by guarantee. Registered in England No. 2931892.

Contents

Acknowledgements

When you focus on a subject for several months in depth, you gain tremendously as you try and think things through from first principles. But you cannot do this in isolation: you test and exchange ideas, you find out what other people have said, and you need a lot of support, encouragement and tolerance. And, of course, whatever you eventually conclude is the result of collation over many years of experience and interaction at every level.

My thanks go first to my colleague Karen Glasse, for her detailed and perceptive research, for significant help with writing the last chapter, and for her helpful comments on the final draft. Geoff Atkinson helped me particularly with the 'eight-step method', and I would like to thank members of the Learning Sharefair network for sharing their own HRD strategies. My assistant, Denise Fordham, finalised the manuscript for me. Finally, I am always conscious of the innovations and professionalism of my ex-colleagues at ICL, and my experiences with them have shaped my view of the HRD world more than any other influence.

There would be no book were it not for the initiative, patience and confidence of Anne Cordwent, my editor. Above all, it is the tolerance and understanding of those who share your life that is essential to a project such as this, and so my final special thanks are to my wife, Elisabeth.

Introduction

Professional HR people are very concerned today to be 'strategic'. A conference session on 'How to link HR with business strategy' will be packed. They are not alone – the same cry comes from IT people and other support functions. They want to feel they have a part in *shaping* the business rather than being mere supporting resources reactive to managerial demands. Above all, there is a desire to be treated as a business partner, sharing in the direction of the organisation.

It may be written one day that the world of corporate priorities changed in 1995. That was the year when the hypothesis that organisations were basically measuring the wrong things gained some momentum. The light dawned that most of an organisation's value was in intangible assets, and that pursuing value growth on the basis of fixed and financial asset management was at best incomplete. The major portion of the intangible asset portfolio concerns people – their capability, their knowledge and their wisdom, and how they are managed and utilised. Growing intangible assets is about growing the stock of capability and knowledge in the organisation. What an exciting and critical role for human resource development! And what a challenge to know just *how* such a mission can be accomplished. Nothing could be more 'strategic'.

It is indeed a changing world, and one that presents a constant challenge to professionals working in human resources to adapt themselves to organisational demands. There are new structures that owe little to the hierarchical model; empowering cultures that see managers in support rather than control; resourcing strategies that are built on flexibility; a much higher profile for and a broader understanding of the meaning of learning; a focus on employability and accreditation; the globalisation of business – just some of the changes that are well known and yet require new and different approaches to people development. The human resource development manager has many more *choices* to make than before, way beyond the identification of training needs and their professional design and delivery.

Strategy, and 'being strategic', are terms both overused and misused in many contexts today, not least in the HR field. It is defined in the 1951 edition of the *Oxford English Dictionary* as 'generalship; the art of war; the management of an army; the art of so moving or disposing troops or ships as to impose upon the enemy the place and time and conditions for fighting preferred by oneself'. No mention of business at all here, although we can logically extrapolate the definition to that of any competitive environment. The implication is that strategy is decided by the top management, and the organisation disposes itself around its achievement. To be 'strategic' is therefore either to be involved in the analysis and choice of options available, and/or to be *supporting* the strategy through the use of resources. It is – at the very least – the latter that we would expect of human resources, but as the realisation grows that people are the ultimate source of value, arguably it has to be the former also.

In many organisations surprisingly little true strategic thinking is done relative to other activities. There are many other processes – business planning, budgeting, reviews and so on – that are to do with *how* the business is operating and that consume energy. Furthermore, the strategies that do exist may be imposed from a remote headquarters, so that practitioners on the ground feel no ownership for it.

Many an HR professional will say, 'I *want* to be strategic, but I don't know how to,' or perhaps, 'I am so busy there is no time to think about the future.'

So how can a book like this be helpful? Hopefully in two ways. The first is to examine the links between business needs – from long-term strategic through current business goals down to solving problems of today's performance – and training and development. The aim is to enable us to *proactively* support the effort towards the organisation's goals, and to ensure all we do is adding value towards their achievement. Second, there are options, choices and decisions to be made about people development – by line management and by those professionally concerned in making it happen. By taking a strategic view, each decision made about people development can be made within a context and be part of a greater whole.

There is undoubtedly a need for a business-oriented and systematic framework to training and development. Despite the welcome recent emphasis on the importance of learning at all levels, there are still many training and development agendas and portfolios that have far more to do with what trainers want to do than with any added value to the organisation. It is very easy to convince oneself and others that a proposed activity is a good thing because time spent in learning of all kinds is likely to produce some benefit. Moreover, people may enjoy their experience. Professional developers by their nature tend to overemphasise 'soft' skill development, believing perhaps that 'task' or 'technical' training will take care of itself. So we have to ask ourselves, 'Are we being driven seriously by identified business needs, or are we coming to our own interpretation of what we think the organisation needs?' This book is dedicated to enabling practitioners to answer positively to the first of these options.

The term 'HRD' will be used as an abbreviation for all activities concerned with training, learning and development, and 'HRDM' to mean the 'human resource development manager'. Whatever the reader's title, hopefully he or she can find a link with this generic term for the professional who is concerned with both doing the right things in training and development, and doing them in the best way. This will often be a generalist HR person whose role includes responsibility for HRD.

The aim of this book, and the *Training Essentials* series of which it forms part, is to be *useful* to practitioners at all levels. This is its only test of success. To be useful in making choices from options, in making decisions about what to do, and in ultimately adding value to their organisations.

2

Thinking about Strategy

Organisational strategy

Millions of words have been written about strategy, and millions of hours spent studying it by executives and MBA students. Some organisations change their strategies with amazing frequency. Others pursue the same mainline directions for years. There are good and mature businesses who would articulate nothing more than 'We are here to make the best return for our shareholders', and will pursue whatever they need to do this. Others have extensive strategic planning departments, and rigorous complex processes that cascade up and down the organisation. Figure 1 on page 6 shows a fairly typical set of steps in the strategic process. Although this depicts a commercial and competitive environment, the same basic steps would apply in the public or voluntary sectors.

The first step is the analysis of an organisation's position in its world. Analytical techniques abound and are continually being invented. Perhaps most tried and trusted of all is the 'SWOT' approach – Strengths, Weaknesses, Opportunities and Threats. Then, based on whatever studies are done, goals are set for achievement. These will typically be about financial factors and market positioning, although 'softer' goals may be set relating to customers and employees. (It is not unknown for these goals to be inconsistent with the analysis, and be fixed for political or 'macho' purposes. 'Aggressive' targets may be more acceptable than realistic ones.) The next step is to choose

Figure 1

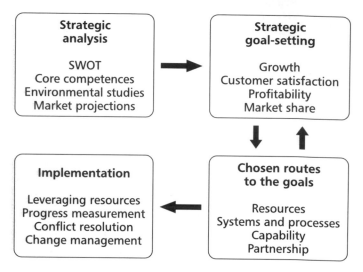

STEPS IN THE STRATEGIC PROCESS

Strategic analysis	Strategic goal-setting
SWOT Core competences Environmental studies Market projections	Growth Customer satisfaction Profitability Market share

Implementation	Chosen routes to the goals
Leveraging resources Progress measurement Conflict resolution Change management	Resources Systems and processes Capability Partnership

routes to the goals. These are the *strategies* – although the word is often used to embrace the goals too. Each requires resources, processes and human capability to make them happen. The reverse arrow represents a *reality check* – is it feasible that we shall achieve what we want with the resources and timescales available? Lastly, all the paper and plans are useless without sound implementation. Indeed, Percy Barnevik, the well-known ex-CEO of ABB, is often quoted as saying 'Strategy is 10 per cent analysis and 90 per cent implementation.' The 's-word' slips off the tongue so readily today that one hears people talk about 'implementation strategies' – meaning ways of making the real strategy actually happen! This may necessitate a revision of the goals.

In most organisations, strategies are generated and decided on by top management, and may be unknown by or have little meaning for the average employee. Hay and Williamson, writing in *Long-range Planning* (October 1997), defined a good strategy seen from *below* as:

- providing inspiration
- helping people see the link between what they are doing and the rest of the company
- offering guidance on trade-offs
- giving people discretion to generate options and act
- helping communication through a common language.

HRD can clearly help in all of these points.

The ultimate test of a coherent strategy is its consistency – externally and internally. A part of that consistency is between short-term actions and long-term goals. It is a useful exercise to ask managers to roughly divide up the way they spend their time – into proactive added-value time that takes the organisation forward towards its goals versus reactive, problem-solving, short-term, internally-focused activity. The result may be an eye-opener and explain why progress on some strategies is so painfully slow.

> Take the opportunity when facilitating workshops or running events to ask managers about the split between the time they spend on short-term problem-solving and on strategic issues to do with the future.

Corporate goals and strategies decided at the top level often do go beyond just quantitative business aims and may include specific statements regarding people, training or development. When they do, it clearly helps both HR and HRD to put together their own strategies, which we shall argue is eventually essential.

Before we go further, we cannot ignore the fact that it may be difficult to actually find any strategies to link into. Some organisations are so short-term (and consistently routine) in their business cycles that life is very 'here-and-now'. In this type of environment, just articulating the strategy as being 'responsive and market-driven' can often help managers and employees to successfully operate.

Others struggle for a long time to find a strategy to choose. If this is the case, it does not mean we cannot have an HRD strategy, since we still have people and have to decide what to do about their development. But we shall need more judgement and intuition in setting priorities than if we can link clearly to business direction.

What involvement could and should HRD have in business strategy?

HR's role in organisational strategy is in helping integration, alignment and understanding. A classic example is the use of reward systems to support (or otherwise) the desired strategies. Many readers will know of cases where sales bonus plans have in fact driven salespeople in quite the opposite direction to that intended by the strategy. Often inappropriate systems live on – perhaps because of their localised ownership – long beyond their useful purpose, because those who maintain them do not see the big picture or think of the longer term. Within HR consistency is needed too. The different parts of the function may not be giving consistent messages, and this we explore in the last chapter.

Undoubtedly a key role for HRD is that of 'educational support to the organisation's strategies' – working to ensure that people understand and can act positively within them. But it can intervene, or be involved, in a number of ways in the strategic process. Table 1 opposite shows different levels of involvement.

When practitioners state the wish to have a 'business-led' training and development strategy, they often mean not more than Levels 10 and 11 in the Table. Their concern is that they should be seen to be directly supportive of the business goals and strategies through their activities and interventions. Since most HRD departments report into a broader HR function, it may be the HR director who is

Table 1

LEVELS OF INVOLVEMENT

LEVEL	INVOLVEMENT
1	Being a member of the strategic analysis group
2	Being part of the team that sets the goals
3	Being part of the team that chooses the business strategies
4	Facilitating meetings or events which analyse the organisation's strategic position
5	Evaluating the strategies for feasibility
6	Monitoring the value of human assets in the organisation and their growth
7	Evaluating the strategies for their human capability requirements, and influencing modifications to the original strategy if necessary
8	Helping the organisation define its general values and approach regarding people development
9	Defining the values and approach of the HRD function regarding people development
10	Choosing the key directions for the HRD strategy
11	Ensuring that people involved have the right knowledge and skills at the right time in order to make the strategies happen

involved in the higher levels – or some of them. Frequently it is the case that he or she is excluded from any input into the substance of the strategies themselves, and is expected only to be involved in implementation. This depends on many factors – cultural, historical, structural – but more than anything else on the calibre and business credibility of the individuals concerned. In Chapter 7 we discuss how credibility and influence can be increased.

> Against these levels make a list of who is involved where in your organisation. Are there any levels not satisfactorily covered? Why is this so? How could this be redressed?

Any influence we seek to bring on the values, the approach or the activities regarding people development should be in the context of how it will help the organisation forward towards its main goals. One might ask why any department would want to spend time and money in ways that would *not* help the organisation towards its goals. The truth is that organisations do a lot of things, consciously or unconsciously, that do not directly take their 'business' forward towards their goals. The philosophy that 'We are doing it because it seems a good thing to do and believe it must be of benefit to the business in the long run' often prevails and survives for years in complacent, relatively wealthy organisations. Trainers are as guilty as anyone of this approach. Not only may they have their own goals and values, but they may be isolated from the business realities and problems. Even when making an effort to seek out the needs of individuals and teams, they may translate them into their preferred comfort zone of solutions. They may be seduced by the positive feedback from their events. They may be keen to experiment with the latest ideas. This is an inappropriate indulgence in organisations under constant pressure to improve value to stakeholders. Every pound or dollar spent on training and development should be linked back to a clear objective that supports the progress of the business. There is one exception: where the organisation deliberately decides to offer areas of personal development to employees as a benefit.

This leads us to a Guiding Principle that we should embrace right at the beginning of our book:

Guiding Principle 1

Rather than compete for senior management time with our own agendas, it is better to see how we can deploy our knowledge, skills and experience in people development to help achieve the goals of senior management.

So we need to be very clear why we choose to spend time and money in a particular way. The expression 'business-led' can be dangerous because of its implication that we should seek a financial benefit in all that we do – and we may waste a lot of effort following trails of evaluation to find answers that in the end will be spurious or inadequate or irrelevant. What we should be clear about is that all our plans and activities are derived from organisational goals – and these may be of varying kinds and with varying periods of time needed for realisation of their benefit. We want to be truly business-oriented in our approach, but realistic in our goals.

The concept of intellectual capital

We have talked about involvement in strategy, but we should briefly divert into an area that fundamentally links HRD and business growth. The concept of intellectual capital is one that every HRDM needs to understand. Organisations today are concerned to grow value – for shareholders, but for customers and other stakeholders too. Value is determined by a stock market, if the organisation is quoted on it, or by estimates of what people would pay for it. In the public sector it is less easy to determine an absolute figure, but it is actually the understanding of the constituents that is more important than accurate and absolute valuation.

The fact that 'intangible assets' cannot be valued accurately has blinded accountants to their importance. The simple equation for calculating them is as follows:

Intellectual capital/Intangible assets = Market value less the tangible assets

The latter are those that appear on the balance sheet. In almost every organisation today the intangible is greater than the tangible. In some, such as Microsoft, it is about 20 times the balance-sheet value.

The most accepted division of these intangible assets is into three categories:

■ customer capital – brands, customer relations, contracts, reputation

■ structural capital – know-how, patents, knowledge, systems, culture

■ human capital – capability, experience, wisdom, and the effectiveness of leadership and organisation.

It is generally very difficult to value separately the constituent components. What is important is to identify them, to understand whether they are increasing and how, and to manage the flows between different categories of capital. 'Human capital' has been defined as 'what leaves the organisation when people go home at night', and it should not be the greatest component (because we want to 'capture' into systems and databases as much of the knowledge and wisdom that people have). The importance of 'knowledge management' becomes clear: the transfer of what resides in people into the structure of the organisation, wherever possible.

Nothing could be more strategic than helping the organisation to grow its intellectual capital. The value-creating chain is shown in Figure 2.

Figure 2

THE VALUE-CREATING CHAIN

This argues that the key to value creation lies in the growth of intangible assets, which is dependent on the growth of knowledge, wisdom and capability in people. An organisation's culture, its use of technology and the power of its processes are enablers of this growth. We could add to these the effectiveness of HRD!

> Identify the main components of intellectual capital in your organisation, especially the human assets. How would you track whether their value was increasing or decreasing? Are some new measures needed?

Clearly HRD should be a fundamental contributor to this chain, provided it is able to link its activities to the addition of value to the organisation through its people.

Terminology

At this point we should define the meanings we shall give to some common words in the training and development arena, namely: *learning*, *capability*, *education*, *training* and *development*.

Learning

Learning is the umbrella term to which all HRD activities belong. Indeed, many former 'training' departments have renamed themselves 'learning and development' or 'learning consultancy'. We shall look at these options later in the book. *Learning*, however, is an end result. It is defined as a change in *capability* whether of individuals, teams or organisational units themselves.

Capability

There are many ways in which capability (this is preferred to 'competency') is defined, but in this book we shall use the following dimensions:

- *behaviour* – the way in which people carry out their organisational roles; the personal skills and personality attributes they deploy
- *know-how* – business, technical and professional knowledge and skills
- *experience* – the diversity of contexts that have been experienced, depth and variety of challenges, successes and failures
- *networks* – the range of contacts, internal and external, that can provide information, expertise and support
- *values and attitudes* – the underlying personality and mindset that drives behaviour.

Education

Tony Miller, co-author of *Measuring the Impact of Training and Development on the Bottom Line*, describes education as mere 'charity'. His point is that we should not expect to see business benefit from everything that goes under the name of training and development. By 'education' we generally mean the broadening or deepening of the knowledge-base of people or groups of people, often accompanied by some form of accreditation.

Education is to do with reframing, refining, or developing the mind, and so also can affect people's attitudes and values. Under this category we would place:

I *many general management development programmes.* These would certainly not come under the heading of 'charitable'. However, they are not aimed at any short-term payoff, and should not be evaluated as such. Whether for individuals or for groups from one organisation, the learning goals are primarily educational – based on our definition. Other benefits are clearly present. Respondents to evaluation questionnaires find the experience very valuable for three reasons: first, the network of people with whom they have shared time; second, the time to reflect on their job; and third, the broadening of their minds giving a sounder basis for future decisions. Organisations use these programmes to create a familiarity with common models and thinking frameworks, to evoke personal insights, to provide dialogue with senior management, or to accelerate change.

I *attitudinal change initiatives.* These would for example include customer orientation, total quality, multicultural awareness, managing diversity – which are educational, but designed to change behaviour within the organisation. To this extent they are more business-linked and should be measurable.

I *achieving professional qualifications.* There are several pressures that encourage this. Customers may specify that they deal only with qualified personnel; governments have national targets and look for co-operation in achieving them; and employees increasingly find an appropriate qualification as a necessary entry passport. Employers may want to encourage study as part of creating an attitude of employability. The actual benefits to the organisation are variable, and we could legitimately class much of what is done in this area of learning as part of the HR benefits strategy rather than of a training and development strategy.

▮ *MBA programmes*. Managers, particularly younger ones, increasingly feel an MBA is a necessary part of their education and employability. Many invest an immense amount of personal time to achieve the goal; for some it is important enough to break employment and do it full-time. Some organisations have created their own customised programme to enable individual aspirations to be met *as well as* to seek some benefit in application to their business.

Training

Training is concerned with know-how, and should be driven by a clearly defined need that is about improving a component of capability. This may come from any of the drivers described below – from a major strategic goal to an individual improvement target. The need may be 'here-and-now' – a requirement for immediate change – or 'postponable' – that is, business-related, important, but with a longer-term payback.

Using the term 'training' does not of course imply traditionally defined programmes or events but involves a range of learning methodologies both within the current job and beyond it.

Development

By 'development' we mean the longer-term investment in people. Development takes time. One does not come back from a leadership course and say, 'Hey! I am now a leader!' What such a course does is to provide a framework for understanding what leadership is about and within which to experiment and act. This requires live, real-time opportunity for the learning to take place. The essence of managing people *development* (whether managed by individuals themselves or with the help of others) is to provide and benefit from life-given opportunities. This implies the management of different kinds of experience such as projects, new roles, promotions, or special team membership.

A model for creating a training and development strategy

The basic model framework we are using is shown in Figure 3, and this book is structured around it. We shall try to use clear terminology that is rigorous and systematic, yet not take a narrow and restricted view of the word 'strategy'. Our goals are firstly to see how HRD can be anchored firmly in the business, and secondly to look at areas of options and decisions that HRD has to make.

Figure 3

A MODEL FOR CREATING AN HRD STRATEGY

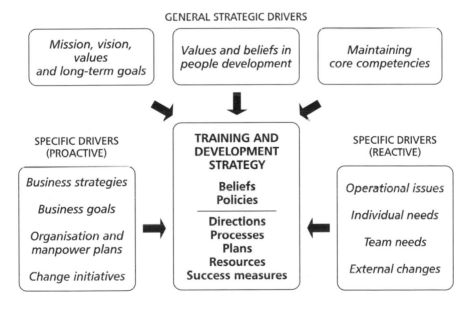

The principle of the model is simple. There are three categories of business or organisational factors that *drive* what our strategy should contain. Understanding the impact of each of these drivers enables us to decide what we should be doing. This is then integrated with our own professional expertise regarding good HRD practice, and hence we formulate policies, processes and plans that comprise our strategy. This has to be implemented, and we need to know it has been done successfully.

> Adapt the model of Figure 3 to your organisation using your own internal language.

What exactly are the driving influences on HRD strategy?
The drivers that are general

The first set of drivers is those that are general – that is, they are more or less permanent and are a support for the ongoing organisation. They represent what it *is* or what it *aims to be*. First will be the mission, vision, and values of the organisation – where stated clearly and publicly. Secondly, we may have a set of values relating specifically to people development. These may or may not be explicit, but they will certainly exist, and will significantly influence our approach to development, as well as certain kinds of training and education. Thirdly, there is the need to maintain, and enhance, what the organisation is really good at doing – its 'core competencies', we might say. Thus if we are in the oil exploration business, we are going to continually focus on generating and sharing knowledge to do with hydrology, drilling technology and production processes because these are fundamental to our business. In a competitive world we may have expertise and methodologies that are closely guarded in these 'core' areas, and we shall probably not want to outsource these.

There is of course nothing in organisations today that can be described as 'permanent'; businesses need to be continually learning and adaptable to change. However, constant changes in direction and approach cause confusion and make it difficult to achieve the benefits that come from many longer-term development programmes. As illustrated clearly in the book *Built to Last* by the

American researchers Porras and Collins (1994), long-term success comes from consistency of vision, beliefs and cultural approaches.

The drivers that are specific

Then there are two sets of more specific drivers – categorised as *proactive* (helping to achieve the future) and *reactive* (dealing with current goals and performance problems). These terms refer to the involvement of the HRDM. *Proactive* implies that learning activities are supporting change, anticipating needs and preparing for the future. This contrasts with being *reactive*, where the HRDM is responding to demands made on him or her. The former type of activities encapsulates where the organisation is going within its planning horizon. The goals and strategies in the current plan all have implications for the capability of divisions, teams and the people in them. Let's say that our goal is to double our sales turnover. How is this going to be achieved? By new products? Or new geographies? Or better salespeople? Or by acquisition? Or by new distribution channels? Whatever the strategy is, people are involved and success or failure depends on their ability to deliver. In addition to overtly business goals the organisation may be planning major change – cultural, structural, or in ways of working. These will certainly require support from HRD.

Current organisational and manpower plans also require proactive action. Many re-organisations are put together with little thought for the capability needed to make them work – until afterwards. Many a workshop on 'matrix management', for example, is remedial. The main goal seems to be to create some semblance of rationality on paper, and slot people into the positions created. The HRDM should ideally be involved in all re-organisations to be able to advise on the capability issues that will need to be addressed. Manpower plans are also critical – beyond headcount figures from the business plans, and focused on flows into, out of and within the organisation. Plans should also define quantities of skills, in the requirements for different skill levels.

Finally, change initiatives of various kinds will always involve HRD. Change programmes by definition seek to create different attitudes, behaviours and skills.

The *reactive* drivers are those arising from everyday processes and work. Performance deficiencies are identified – at any level, from organisation-wide to the individual employee. HRD is rightly required to respond to these in an appropriate manner. External changes arise also which demand a response – changes in regulations, in the law, or other factors in the environment in which the organisation operates.

Taken together, these drivers define the possible portfolio of contributions that HRD can make. The strategic HRDM will be aware of the risks of HRD determining its own agenda – built from courses it has always run, from areas that are fashionable or enjoyable to trainers, or from some kind of 'training needs analysis' that may be little more than a summary of appraisal outputs, themselves conditioned by the catalogue that is sent from the training department. Indeed, there are dangers in some forms of 'TNA', if we start with such questions as 'What do you see as the training needs of your team/self, etc?' (Readers are referred to the companion volume in this series, *Identifying Training Needs*, by T. Boydell and M. Leary, London, IPD, 1996.)

It is not surprising that many struggle with issues such as evaluation and effectiveness. The problem is that we often start in the wrong place. It is right to measure whether any activity is successful in meeting its goals, of course, but we may formulate a second Guiding Principle:

Guiding Principle 2

There will never be a problem in evaluating the effectiveness of training if the objectives and design were derived from a genuine business-driver in the first place.

Chapter 3 discusses these drivers in more detail and shows how we can derive learning goals from them.

The professional management of HRD

The drivers tell HRD what needs to be achieved through learning. How are we going to make it all happen? In 1988 the Ashridge Management Research Group distinguished three basic models of managing HRD with progressive levels of sophistication:

▉ *the fragmented approach* – an emphasis on training programmes, discrete and formalised, and unconnected particularly with business priorities

▉ *the formalised approach* – a more professional systematisation of training activities, including pre- and post-event activities

▉ *the focused approach* – where training and development is a tool of organisational success, and activities are clearly focused towards that end.

This book is essentially about the last approach, but we should remind ourselves that the HRDM has to make choices at this level: what kind of a function is he or she going to run?

HRD has its own internal strategies: choices it has to make about how it will position itself and operate. It needs its own set of approaches and principles. The department will be responsible for designing and maintaining processes aimed at specifying needs, setting learning objectives, defining solutions, and evaluating outcomes. Such processes will determine the roles of different parties involved in making things happen in training and development. Finally, no strategy is complete without indicators of performance, achievement, and effectiveness by which progress will be judged.

Chapter 4 looks at the management of HRD as a function.

HRD policies

If 'strategy' is to be confused with anything, it often overlaps with 'policy'. However, it is strategies that help decide what the policy should be. Policies exist to enable others to make decisions. Some organisations allow more discretion than others, but the minimum purpose is to lay down the basic rules of guidance consistent with the organisation's HRD principles, and to encourage managers and employees to make decisions within them. Policies will vary in relation to the levels of authority and discretion given.

Many policies in education, training and development will be organisation-wide. Others will apply to certain subgroups only. It helps to see the organisation as a series of 'families', each with its own characteristics and requirements. Such families might include:

Senior management	Other management
Technical/professional experts	Administrative support
Potential general managers	Front-line operating staff
Young entrant trainees	Peripheral (non-core) staff

Aspects of policy are discussed in Chapter 5.

Making it happen

Finally, with all the above in place, we can get on with formulating the strategy and making it happen. Taking all the business drivers into account, plus the professional HRD overlay, we are able to set the basic directions that should be followed. These directions are the core of our plans. Making them happen is not really a part of strategy (although as noted earlier it is 90 per cent of the added value!) and is covered well elsewhere in the IPD's *Training Essentials* series. It includes the setting of HRD goals, putting together training plans, the choice of resources, options for learning methodologies and evaluation systems. However, there are some 'strategic choices' to be made, especially in terms of resources – in terms of people, organisation, facilities and equipment, and whether we are going to own and manage any of these.

These are discussed in Chapter 6.

The last chapter is devoted to the political aspects of HRD. Reaching out to all levels and all units, the HR department is inevitably pulled in different directions. How does it choose who and where it needs to influence in the organisation? How does it position and market its services?

Strategy documentation

At the end of this section, we outline some actual organisational strategy documents, and they are very diverse. We need to be clear about:

■ *the purpose* – why we are doing it and what it will be used for

■ *the audience* – who will see it and what message we want to convey

■ *the format* – what will be included

■ *the process of creation* – how we shall put it together.

The purpose

Many organisations could not explain their strategy but could produce various documents that describe things that they do in HRD, and the part that managers or employees should play in development. Why take the trouble to produce a comprehensively documented strategy? There are a number of possible reasons:

- as part of an organisational strategic planning process which requires a set of coherent, integrated strategies from all activities – including HR/HRD
- as a vehicle for consultation/discussion with line management about training and development issues
- as a means of communicating beliefs, policies and plans to staff
- for managing expectations in people development
- as a means of linking HRD activities systematically with business needs
- for establishing priorities and plans for HRD activities and resources
- for achieving an approved and authoritative framework for HRD policies and activities
- as a means of 'zero-basing' current activity and recalibrating what HRD is doing and how it is doing it
- for securing budgets and resources
- for demonstrating to external bodies that required standards are being met
- for influencing change
- for internal visibility and credibility
- for providing integration across disparate units
- for external publicity.

It is highly likely that one or more of these reasons exists, and that disciplined systematic thinking and presentation will achieve the particular goal that is sought.

Who it is for

All communications should be tailored to their audience. Who they are addressed to will depend on their purpose. An HRD strategy may have several different audiences. Table 2 shows some of them, with possible goals of communication, and the consequent emphasis on content.

Table 2

AUDIENCES FOR A STRATEGY DOCUMENT

Type of audience	Goals of communication	Content emphasis
Chief executives	Commitment, involvement	Executive summary, business links, personal commitments needed
HR directors	Approval, resources	Business links, professional methodology, resources, costs
Strategic planners	Process completion	Meeting requirements, links to business and other strategies
Line managers	Involvement, partnership	Processes, roles, involvement
HRD staff	Commitment, participation	Priorities, skills
All employees	Information, participation	Policies, directions, plans
Operational HR staff	Support, co-operation	Processes, roles, involvement
Trade union/staff reps	Support, co-operation	Investment in people
External assessors	Approval	Meeting standards required
External committees	Approval	Meeting external interest
Fund providers	Approval, resources	Meeting funds criteria
Other organisations	Publicity, image, reputation	Professionalism, leading-edge practices

Thus our actual document might have various modules aimed at these audiences. It is unlikely to be helpful to send the full strategy to everyone. A summary at the front should address any concerns the audience are likely to have, their own interests, and the key messages or commitments that HRD wants from them.

> What purposes and which audiences exist in your organisation for an HRD strategy? List them in approximate order of priority.

The format of a strategy document

Many a corporate function has invested an immense amount of time in producing magnificently bound documents which are duly circulated and thud into pending-trays, or which come as lengthy e-mails which try the patience of their recipients. A large part of a strategy should be semi-permanent and not need renewal more frequently than that of the organisation's strategic plan. Before we assume we need just one document, it is worth noting another Guiding Principle.

Guiding Principle 3

It may be better to have a series of separate documents that meet the varied purposes and audiences that we have identified who have a stake in our strategy.

Table 3, opposite, shows the possible constituents of a training and development strategy.

Table 3

HEADINGS FOR A TRAINING AND DEVELOPMENT STRATEGY DOCUMENT

1   Executive summary

2   Statement of purpose

3   Statement of organisational beliefs concerning people development

4   Organisational mission, vision, goals and core competences

5   How HRD will support them

6   HRD policy framework

7   Principles governing the HRD department; own mission statement if desired

8   Ways of working, standards of performance and measures of success for HRD

9   Main business goals and strategies, and their implications for learning and development

10   Meeting external standards

11   Changes in the external environment that require a response

12   Strategic goals for HRD

13   Major priority activities in the coming period

14   Resources needed

15   Roles and responsibilities

These headings may not all be necessary in one document. Arguably, however, they should be found *somewhere* – that is, HRD must have thought through all these issues and worked out where it should be.

Creating the strategy document

The HRDM should take the Model in Figure 3 (see page 17) and go systematically through the various components. (A methodology for taking business goals and evaluating the associated learning goals is described in Chapter 3, and this needs considerable consultancy skills.) It will not be necessary to study every component every year, especially the 'general drivers', but all should be done at some point.

The process of building up the strategy may be used as a powerful intervention in the organisation's thinking about people development. Most managers do not give a lot of daily thought to this area of organisational life. So for the HRDM (or his or her delegate) to hide away in a corner and produce a magnificent document may be satisfying, but it represents a missed opportunity. Mechanisms for involving others include:

■ asking top management teams to articulate their beliefs about people development (see instrument in Table 7)

■ discussion and involvement with corporate strategic planning departments

■ focus groups with cross-sections of staff

■ meetings with HR professionals in business units

■ discussions with individual line management or line management teams about business priorities and performance issues

■ 'If you were HRD Manager, what would be your priorities?' – interviews, discussion or questionnaires with different groups.

Such dialogues should always start with a 'bridge' to what is important for the individual or group concerned. Discussion can then be steered towards HRD's agenda.

> Think of some areas (or people) that seem to have less interest in the role and activities of HRD than others. What is particularly important to them, and therefore what methods could you use to get them more involved?

What do actual strategy documents look like?

Some research was carried out to see what a cross-section of organisations actually had by way of documentation. A number that were contacted said with some embarrassment that they did not have any or were 'working on it'. However, some examples were impressive.

W H Smith

At the corporate level, this firm has a Learning and Development Policy. It comprises two pages and outlines the company's approach at the three levels of the organisation, the line manager and the individual. Each section has a few statements of belief (eg 'We wish to encourage in all employees a lifetime habit of learning') and a description of responsibilities. A very clear emphasis is placed on individual responsibility – and the line manager is expected to be a role model in this.

HSBC

This organisation's strategy document starts with an introduction that restates the company's 'People Strategy Objectives' for three years ahead. Chapter 2 is entitled 'Goals and Objectives', and names one overriding goal as *Investment in learning for all our people and our business to enable them to grow and prosper together*. Nine objectives follow: a mixture of longer-term cultural goals and specific programmes to be delivered. A third section follows which lists nine priorities. This is then backed up by a detailed implementation plan, and finally a list of roles and responsibilities.

British Airports Authority

BAA has a Strategy for Training and Learning. It starts by outlining a 'Vision' ('Our people will be the best in our industry worldwide and they will be the principle source of competitive advantage') and Mission, and has three 'Major Goals' for its Strategy:

- creating and maintaining an effective business process for training investment
- providing excellent programmes and services which meet the training and development needs of the business
- encouraging employees to adopt the habit of continuous learning.

The strategy document goes on to specify key goals for the coming year, critical success factors, costs, indicators of success, and benchmarking plans. The three major goals have their action plans for achievement attached as an appendix.

Hertfordshire County Council

This council has a Corporate Training and Development Strategy in the form of a four-page handout, clearly and professionally printed. Its overall strategy is defined under three 'Beliefs':

- The development of all our staff is central to the achievement of the Council's strategic intent.
- We shall support people so that they welcome and can cope with the changes which we need to make. This will underpin all our development activities.
- Success will only be achieved by releasing and realising the potential of the people we employ.

The context of change is described, and a number of specific ones enumerated. This then leads to five key issues which form the basis of the strategy:

- how to create a development and learning culture within the Council
- how to develop managers for the future
- how to respond to the County Agenda (the County Council's overall strategy)
- how to develop staff to meet the demands of competition
- how to respond to the national targets for education and training and to NVQs.

Finally actions – and in some cases policies – are listed for each of these five issues. (See Appendix to this book.)

Barclaycard

Entitled 'Training and Development – A Strategy for Developing People', this document states at the beginning that the strategy sets out to address four key issues:

- the need to relate training to business results
- the need for continuous development of people
- the need to develop the organisation's capability to manage change
- the need to develop and harness exceptional people.

These are expanded upon in brief paragraphs, followed by the heading 'Main Elements of the Strategy'. These are four 'complementary strands':

- managing for performance (a new system to be introduced)
- self-managed learning
- change management capability (emphasis on ensuring that the capabilities necessary for specific change implementations are present)
- the talent pool (building it up more systematically and growing individuals in it).

Resources and costs that will be needed are enumerated, and comparisons made with current activities – explaining how resource allocation will change. The document concludes with an overview of implementation plans.

BT

Perhaps typical of many companies, BT describes the various components of its training and development activities as a series of policies and processes in one document for employees under the title of 'The Partnership'. It presents its beliefs, approaches and activities in a context of 'what we offer' and 'how you can play a part'. Free-standing leaflets on particular processes are contained in a pocket within a covering folder, together with references to the extensive material available on BT Internet.

As part of the strategic planning process, an annual 'people strategy' is included. However, this does not change too much from year to year and tends to reiterate the main guiding approaches to people development. Whereas approaches to development strategies tend to be centralised and common, training delivery is responsive to the needs of various divisions and determined by them.

A leading financial services company

This company has an overall development strategy based on the learning organisation model described by A. Mayo and E. Lank in *The Power of Learning* (London, IPD, 1994).

A team of senior executives identified six key business processes used as drivers for the major strands of HRD strategy. These strands are explained on a 'two by two' diagram, one axis being 'Organisation/Individual' and the other 'Today/Tomorrow'; within each quadrant are key HRD activities. Thus the quadrant 'Tomorrow/Individual' includes career management and succession planning. The quadrants are built around a central core that includes values, behaviours and performance management.

Frizzell

This company with a high reputation for training has a policy statement on training and development as follows:

> The Group aims to ensure that all members of staff have the knowledge, skills and experience necessary to be successful in their jobs and to fulfil their career potential. Opportunities, facilities and financial help are available to assist staff in achieving this goal. The Group believes that learning is a lifelong process and employees should embrace this philosophy and share in the responsibility for their own development.

The simple two-page document goes on to to explain some specific policies on coaching, work experience, NVQs, external education, etc.

Lifecare National Health Trust

The Trust has a one-and-a-half page section as part of its 'Personnel Strategy'. The introduction has a couple of sentences regarding commitment to training in the Trust's core competence and building on its IIP award. There are then seven short paragraphs describing priority training activities and processes.

Johnson & Johnson

This healthcare company has a document entitled 'Training and Development Strategy'. It begins with 'Benefits of an Employee Training Strategy', which has eight bullet points. There follows a 'Mission' and a 'Policy Statement'. ('The company will ensure that each employee is trained to carry out the tasks required of him/her. Further, the company will encourage each employee to develop his/her skills consistent with the needs of customer-driven continuous improvement and his/her own individual needs and aspirations'.) There follows a 'Summary of the Relationship Between Business Strategy and Employee Training Strategy', a summary of the links and the drivers, and then 'Seven Steps of the Employee Training Strategy'. These are in fact steps in systematic training management. 'Roles in Training' comes next, followed by 'Eight Objectives of the Training and Development Strategy'.

Zeneca

The company has articulated eight strands of a 'People Development Strategy', which constitute (in the language we have been using) its beliefs. Included in these are:

- Employees are our single most important asset, and we shall have a *business* objective 'to ensure a well-motivated organisation in which people are respected, enjoy their jobs and obtain fulfilment'. This policy relates to *all* employees.
- Expenditure on education, training and development is regarded as a necessary and calculated investment.
- Performance management is the preferred integrated approach that brings together work activities and development plans.
- All employees must have a personal development plan jointly agreed with their manager.
- Career planning will be a joint activity between the individual and the manager.
- The business requires core competence in team-building, project management and cross-cultural management skills.
- People development activities will be regularly audited to ensure that cost-effective investments are supporting business priorities.

Further case-studies

In 1988 a volume entitled *Successful Training Strategies* was published by Jill Castner-Latto and associate authors. Its subtitle is 'How leading companies are reshaping their training strategies', and it groups 26 company studies under five headings:

- aligning training strategy with corporate goals
- continuous learning for all employees
- manufacturing–user training partnerships
- designing and delivering training cost-effectiveness
- combining continuous learning and employment security.

Although American and somewhat dated, it has a wealth of practical examples of different approaches taken to meet organisational and individual goals.

A survey by *Training* magazine in March 1998 of a number of training directors regarding the key changes in HRD showed that the priorities occupying their minds were very much business-driven and were quite different from those of a few years ago. Devolution of training management to line managers and individuals themselves featured strongly, along with extensive outsourcing of resources, creating a pervasive learning environment, the growth of the learning consultant role, and the management of learning beyond the classroom.

> What form of documentation would meet the needs of your organisation and be consistent with its culture? Draw up a specification for the headings you would use in the documents you choose.

In brief

- There are many methods and approaches to business strategy, but a fundamental question is the extent to which people and their capabilities are taken into account in the planning process. We might have some different strategies and goals if we did so.

- Eleven possible levels of strategic involvement by HRD were identified. The question for the reader is 'Where *am* I involved, and where *should* I be involved?'

- A fundamental strategic imperative in growing value in organisations is to grow the *intellectual capital*, the source of which resides in people, their capability and potential, and how they are led and organised. One could have no greater strategic impact on an organisation than to be instrumental in this growth.
- We defined learning as being a change in capability. This may be achieved through education, training or development – and HRD is concerned with all of these.
- The core of this book is a systematic model for creating a strategy, driven by the organisation's goals and issues. HRD lends its own professionalism to deciding how learning can be effective, and to deriving policies and processes that enable it to be successful.
- What would a strategy look like? It depends on the purpose(s) and audience(s). We may have several components or versions, consistent with one another but designed to communicate the right messages to their recipients.

3

The Drivers of HRD Strategy

Our basic model for building an HRD strategy was described in Figure 3. It outlines the drivers of a strategy, and distinguishes between the *general* and the *specific*.

What are the general drivers of HRD strategy?

The general drivers are semi-permanent, in that they have some stability and continuity and are about what the organisation *is* or what it *wants to be*. Many organisations go to great lengths to refine statements of one kind or another; others do nothing at all. However, if they exist and are to be taken seriously, then HRD must ask how they are going to be supported and made into the intended reality.

Mission, vision, values and long-term goals

Mission and vision statements can be both confused and confusing. At worst, they can be convoluted lengthy paragraphs; alternatively they can be banal, meaningless dreams that have little grasp on the hearts and minds of employees.

A mission statement should describe *what business we are in* or *what we are*. It should not of itself include grand goals and ambitions, but be clear and simple.

Examples from world-class companies and international organisations include:

Motorola Statement of Purpose

> The purpose of Motorola is to honorably serve the community by producing products and services of superior quality at a fair price to our customers; to do this so as to earn an adequate profit which is required for the enterprise to grow; and by so doing provide the opportunity for our employees and shareholders to achieve their reasonable personal objectives.

Merck

> We are in the business of preserving and improving human life. All of our actions must be measured by our success in achieving this goal.

Hewlett Packard Statement of Purpose

> To create Information Products that accelerate the advancement of knowledge and fundamentally improve the effectiveness of people and organisations.

Disney

> We exist to bring happiness to millions.

The Girl Guides Association

> To help a girl reach her highest potential.

Virgin Atlantic

> As the UK's second-biggest long-haul carrier, to build an intercontinental network concentrating on those routes with a substantial established market and clear indication of growth potential, by offering the highest possible service at the lowest possible cost.

Readers can form their own judgements about the worth of these. The comic-strip character Dilbert describes mission statements as 'a long and awkward statement that demonstrates management's inability to think clearly'. But if we can get a clear statement, it will help to define the major core competences needed to make the organisation a winner in its field. These are discussed further below.

Confusion may be caused by divisions and departments creating their own statements and thus causing people difficulty in knowing which they should identify with. HRD should be clear which statements it is expected to reinforce or help to achieve.

Further direction may be given through *vision statements, statements of direction, corporate goals/objectives* and *corporate strategies*. These are distinguished from purpose and values by being time-related. At a corporate level they may be very general and described in overall bottom-line terms. As they are cascaded through business units they become more detailed and (should) affect the work of units, teams and individuals.

A *vision statement* targets a long-term goal. It needs to be achievable but so stretching that it cannot be conceived of being reached in the short term. Hamel and Prahalad used the words 'strategic intent', which seems to convey the sense of vision well. Perhaps the most famous stated goal of all was that of Komatsu in the 1970s, which was simply 'Kill Caterpillar!' All employees saw this on the doormat as they entered work every day, and there was no difficulty in either remembering or embracing it. It was a part of everyday life. By contrast, others have long-winded paragraphs that have clearly been put together by committees. The benefit of a vision is shown simply in the following examples, for if employees can see the big picture, they will do their part with an understanding of the system to which they belong.

> *Three stone-cutters were asked about their jobs.*
>
> *The first said that he was paid to cut stones.*
>
> *The second replied that he used special techniques to shape stones in an exceptional way, and proceeded to demonstrate his skills.*
>
> *The third stone-cutter just smiled and said, 'I build cathedrals.'*

By contrast, this parody of vision statements illustrates the same point:

> **Evolution of a vision statement by a cathedral builder**
>
> *We are building a great cathedral.*
>
> *Our aim is to build the greatest cathedral in Christendom, to the greater glory of God.*
>
> *By striving to become Europe's leading construction group, we aim to build a cathedral that offers value for money as well as spiritual enhancement for worshippers, is environmentally healthy, and will generate handsome returns on the investment in terms of increased attendance at services and associated increases in revenues.*

Examples of various company vision statements – some not really distinguishable from the type of mission statement exampled above – include:

Guinness

To be the world's leading marketer of quality alcoholic drinks through a world-class portfolio of international brands.

Bell Atlantic

To be the world's best communications, information and entertainment company.

Bridgestone

To be the number one tyre manufacturer in the world.

GE Appliances

One team, faster than anyone else in the world.

Waste Management Technologies

To be the acknowledged worldwide leader in providing comprehensive environment, waste management and related services of the highest quality to industry, government and consumers, using state-of-the-art systems responsive to customer need, sound environmental policy and the highest standards of corporate citizenship.

In order for people to identify with such a vision, and find it helpful, it needs to be focused, measurable, and at some point realistically achievable. Statements that refer just to being 'the best' or 'number one' or 'the leading company' in an arena need to be qualified. Leading *how* – in size, quality, service, innovation? Best in *what*? If we do not know that, we cannot have any sense of where we are in relation to the end goal and what kind of gaps we have to close to achieve it.

The vision should be the ultimate goal (as we see it today) and should be the apex of a pyramid of cascaded goals. All the different organisational measures should ultimately contribute to this end goal. In practice, it is almost impossible to break down a visionary long-term goal into precise components for everyone. But:

Guiding Principle 4

Individuals should each be able to say how their role and their key goals contribute to the corporate vision.

What about organisational values?

In continuing to describe what kind of organisation we would like to be, we may support our mission statement with a statement of *business philosophy and/or values*. Values help to articulate a philosophy and standards of behaviour that should characterise the way the company and its people operate. They provide part of the 'corporate glue' and common language that binds a diverse corporation together and makes the corporate name stand for something in the world of business. Values may be encapsulated in a booklet that lays them out systematically, perhaps with a set of *management principles* as well, and termed *'The [organisation's] Way'*. Hewlett Packard was probably the originator of this approach, and many have followed in their footsteps. Thus we have 'The Nokia Way', 'The ICL Way', 'The Philips Way'.

Porras and Collins in *Built to Last* emphasise very strongly the value of a core ideology, which they define as 'core values' + 'purpose'. Core values are defined as 'the organisation's essential and enduring tenets – a small set of guiding principles; not to be confused with specific cultural or operating practices; not to be compromised for financial gain or short term expediency'. They are permanent. One of the tests to be made is whether the *written* and *unwritten* values of 'what is actually acceptable around here' actually match. Often this is not the case…and where there are written values it is always useful to test the unwritten ones against them from time to time.

Ricardo Semler in his book *Maverick* – which describes how, as a CEO, he turned traditional management thinking on its head – asserts that organisations cannot have values: only people do. Nevertheless, the people in an organisation can work together, and act towards their customers or public to some common standards of behaviour. Stated values, discussed, understood and adopted, can help guide that behaviour. Again, attempts to create values often fail because there are too many to remember, they are too vague to be meaningful, or they lack reinforcement of any significant kind in the daily life of the organisation. Worst of all, top management does not take them seriously in their decisions. They become no more than a wish-list without a coherent plan to make them a living reality.

Values may be used as a yardstick for challenging individual or organisational behaviour, for clarifying expectations, for guiding decisions and resolving conflicting demands, and in establishing reputation and image. When subsidiary business units design their own set of values, they will take precedence over the corporate ones, if they exist. Unless they are *additions* to the corporate set, this does create confusion and negates their original purpose.

> Look for opportunities to test individuals at different levels on their memory of organisational mission, vision and value statements, and their ability to describe what they mean to them personally in their everyday work. Be open to the messages the results may give regarding HRD's role in helping them to do so.

Table 4

THE DANA CORPORATION'S 'TEN KEY THOUGHTS'

Dana people serve the shareholder

Dana people are our most important asset

Dana people accept only total quality

Dana people discourage centralisation

Dana people do what's best for all of Dana

Dana people participate and innovate

Dana people compete globally

Dana people focus on the customer

Dana people communicate fully

Dana people are good citizens

It is always an important test of the currency and meaning of corporate values to see how many people can recite them. Often they were produced in an era of enthusiasm for renewal, or by a previous management team, and they have lost their significance in current everyday life. Companies with strong cultures invest time in every new employee to help him or her to understand their values and ways of working. Table 4 above shows one example – from the Dana Corporation in the USA.

These statements have enormous implications for the culture, processes and capabilities in the Dana Corporation. How would HRD support sets of values? Firstly, HRD should seek to be a role model in putting them into practice itself. Secondly, the values should guide our beliefs about people development. Thirdly, we should follow through the eight steps described below and see how we can help people be *competent* in their application. Use learning opportunities to make them a living reality. Let's take 'teamwork' as an example. What exactly do we expect to see when 'teamwork' is alive and well and a feature of our behavioural landscape? We would define process and behavioural characteristics of teams and individuals. We would devise a measuring instrument that can test the reality (through collecting perceptions). The gaps between reality and ideal will help set our learning objectives.

> If you have a set of values explicit in your organisation, which of your programmes and events directly support one or more of them? How does HRD live the values through its own ways of operating?

How do we derive learning goals from business drivers?

We can easily assent to the role of HRD in supporting the business drivers. The question is 'How?' We cannot escape from the need to have a solid understanding of business in general and a genuine interest (ideally plus experience) in the challenges of the particular organisation to which we belong. Our model in Figure 3 has five arrows that actually are fundamental to it.

How do we make the critical link between a business driver and the learning goals that will support it? Figure 4, overleaf, shows a flow diagram of a series of steps that are generally applicable for linking training and development to business goals, and also for determining where training can help the solving of operational problems. It aspires to provide the 'missing link' between being truly business-led and the professional application of learning.

The 'eight-step method'

The 'eight-step method' has the following features:

∎ It focuses on the importance of *quantification* of goals or performance gaps.

∎ It involves understanding the business drivers that affect the desired end state, both positively and negatively.

Figure 4

FROM BUSINESS GOALS TO LEARNING GOALS IN EIGHT STEPS

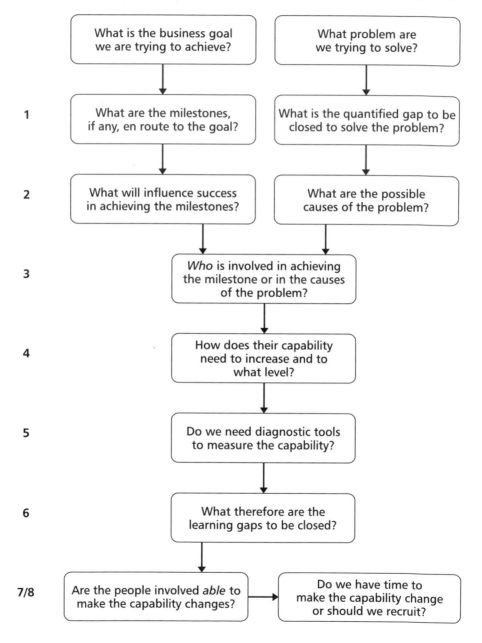

■ It embraces all those who *influence* those drivers.

■ It encourages the clear definition of *capability levels* as learning goals, and the use of appropriate measuring instruments for them.

■ It does not assume there is a *training* solution.

■ It does not assume that everyone *can achieve* the desired level of capability.

This methodology, or something similar, is vital for HRD practitioners, so we explore it in a little more detail.

1 For any given goal, what are the milestones, if any, towards its achievement? Without milestones, many strategies and goals can serve as little more than wish-lists or dreams, and their chance of being achieved will be low. Effort and resources must be dedicated, and that requires progress towards the goal to be built into the action plans of individuals. A milestone is simply a measurable statement of what we want to have achieved at the end of a planning period.

2 *How* will this milestone be achieved or performance gap closed? What are the influencing factors that need to be managed to ensure success? Milestones are not achieved through the mere passing of time. They require action – and this critical step is about looking at the causal influences that affect achievement one way or the other. We can identify positive forces (both external and internal) that should be strengthened, negative ones that can be reduced or eliminated, and there may be completely new initiatives to be taken.

3 *Who* (the whole organisation, subgroups and/or individuals) is involved in causing change? It is people who design and implement processes and are involved in every aspect of change. This step identifies all those who have some responsibility for and/or involvement in the factors outlined in the previous step.

4 What components of their capability (skills, knowledge, personal capabilities, experience, networks, values and

attitudes) drive the factors above, and what is the level we need? It is highly likely that achieving the milestone will be dependent on a *new* level of capability in individuals and/or groups. We may in some cases need change in the whole organisation. We need to define the level(s) of capability needed for success. Appropriate 'capability frameworks' can assist us considerably.

5   Do we need any diagnostic tools to determine the level of that capability? There will be situations where the present level of capability may not be at all clear. For example, one of our strategic goals may be to 'create a more open, blame-free learning culture'. We may have an intuitive feel of how it is today, but in order to help the change some clearer analysis is going to help us. So we may need to create some measuring instruments that can assess 'gaps' and the progress made in closing them.

6   What therefore are the learning objectives that need to be set in order to close the learning gaps we have identified? This is the vital step that will lead us in the systematic learning process. Objectives should follow the 'SMART' acronym (Specific, Measurable, Agreed, Realistic, and Time-Related) and be behavioural in the sense of describing visible changes in behaviour as a result of the learning.

7   How sure are we that the individuals concerned have the capability to make the changes? This is a sensitive area, and the truth is that we may not be sure at all. More often than not, we give people the benefit of the doubt, and consequently waste time and money and frustrate people as they realise their inability to cope. Wherever possible, we should assess aptitude for the change in capability needed.

8   Do we have the time to make the capability changes, or should we recruit or subcontract for them? Whether the aptitude is there or not, it could still be the case that some changes will take a long time to achieve, especially if they are attitude or experience objectives.

Our milestone may be achieved faster by buying in the capability we need – although this may have undesirable side-effects, and the answer might be to revise the milestone itself.

These eight steps prepare us for following through the systematic training described in the companion books in this *Training Essentials* series.

Different types of learning goal

In Step 6, the nature of the learning objectives will depend on the original driver we are supporting, and this will affect the level of evaluation of the eventual learning.

Table 5 shows how they vary. Not every learning goal has a measurable quantitative outcome, even though it is expected to eventually contribute to one. Learning goals should be set so they can be realistically measured.

Table 5

TYPES OF LEARNING GOAL

Driver	Types of learning goals
Mission	Core competence levels of expertise
Vision	Bottom-line, cultural and behavioural measures, levels of expertise
Values	Behavioural measures
Core competences	Levels of expertise
Business goals and strategies	Bottom-line measures
Organisation plans	Capability measures
Manpower plans	Capability, retention, development ratios
Organisational change	Bottom-line, cultural and behavioural measures
Operational performance	Quantitative business measures
Individual performance	Capability measures
Team performance	Quantitative business measures, team effectiveness, productivity
External change	Capability measures

The eight steps in practice

The practical process for applying the method would entail the following:

▮ The learning consultant would prepare for the discussion by finding out as much as possible about the business unit to be studied, and by having to hand any descriptions of capability that are relevant or any appropriate diagnostic tools.

▮ He or she would prepare some working sheets in advance, modelled on Table 6, on page 53.

▮ The consultant either leads a structured discussion with representatives of the unit concerned, or conducts an interview with the manager of the unit.

▮ The aim at this stage is to get to Step 5.

▮ It may be necessary to create some diagnostics or measures if no suitable ones are available.

▮ Step 6 may take some time, as the diagnostics are applied to relevant groups and individuals in order to determine capability gaps. Some self- and peer assessment may be needed in addition to managerial judgement. At the end of this, we come out with a set of learning objectives.

▮ We do Steps 7 and 8 and, on the assumption we want to go ahead, we then check on any practical constraints of time and money before moving into selecting the best way of achieving the learning goals.

A worked example

Let us suppose we have this vision statement:

' To be recognised as the most innovative company in our business sector with greater than 15 per cent market share in every one of our geographic markets.'

Step 1

We cannot set milestones without knowing where we are today. The second goal is easier to measure than the first – let us assume that the data is available and we have a common understanding of which market 'share' we are talking about. The first goal requires a measure to be chosen for innovation. What do we mean by 'most innovative'? How will it be measured? Are we talking products, marketing or organisation? Who shall we compare against, and is the data available? How far behind are we now (if at all)? What is our catch-up target for the next year?

Perhaps the most commonly used milestone is the percentage of sales that comes from products/services introduced in, say, the last three years (the figure depends on the nature of the business). So, if our planning period is 12 to 18 months from now, how much of the total gap would we target to close in that time?

Step 2

This step requires consultancy skills and reasonable business knowledge. What factors will influence these goals? Innovation targets will be influenced by: a culture of experimentation; the level of creativity of some staff groups; the environment; allocation of resources; sensitivity to market needs; time to market and logistics capability; product promotion and marketing…among others! What is going to make us *more* innovative than we are? Is anything working against us?

For the marketing goals, in each geographical market, what drives market share today (products, price, promotion, distribution, reputation, sales resources…)? What strategies from competitors may work against us?

We can see immediately that we shall generate a number of separate 'paths' to follow, and the more general the goal, the more people will be potentially contributing to it. A spreadsheet format is going to help us as we go through this analysis, and the example is taken further in Table 6, opposite.

Guiding Principle 5

Without a logical sequence of steps to go through, we may find our links to the business are random, unprioritised and built on assumptions that may not be valid.

By contrast, below is a parody of an approach that is all too common, creating an illusion of being business-linked but containing wildly assumptive leaps from step to step:

We have a problem of falling sales and market share.

= Management is clearly not doing a good job.

= We need better managers and leaders.

= We'd better do some leadership training.

= We'll use a competency framework for 360-degree assessment.

= We'll design a programme around the major gaps we find.

Try applying the eight-step method to the mission, vision and one or two value statements that you have in your organisation. You will need to follow one path at a time. (It will help to create your own spreadsheet.) Does the exercise reveal any gaps that either HRD or the line are not addressing?

Table 6

DERIVING LEARNING GOALS FROM BUSINESS GOALS – AN EXAMPLE

Vision: 'To be recognised as the most innovative company in our business sector with greater than 15% market share in every one of our geographic markets.'

Measures: 'The percentage of sales attributable to products introduced in the last three years; market share by country of sales per annum.'
Milestones (18 months from now): *Innovation* – to go from current 12% to 18%. *Market share* – to go from average 9% to average 12%.

Influencing factors (Innovation)	People involved	Capabilities needed	Measures?	Learning goals	Capability?	Time?
1 Market sensitivity	Salespeople	Run focus groups with customers	✓	To enable 50% of salespeople to run effectively by April	✓	✓
	Marketing managers	Benchmark innovation in other companies	✓	To understand and implement effective benchmarking methodology	✓	✓
		To be able to take customer needs and translate them into product/service ideas	✗	To improve creativity of marketing teams	?	?
		To understand better goals and vision of key customers	✓	Understanding and application of 'customer activity cycles' for at least one member per marketing team	✓	✓
2 Culture of experimentation in R&D	R&D managers	Encourage non-prescribed experiments	✓	OK at present – no requirement		
3 Logistics capability to deal with expanding production-line complexity	Logistics managers	Complex scheduling and optimum warehousing	✓	They have the capability, but there is a systems problem		
	IT management	Understanding of strategic vision	✗	To enable IT managers to align priorities for resources with strategy	✓	✓
4 Attitude towards innovation in support functions	Accountants	Flexibility of budgeting processes to allow for innovative opportunities to be seized	✓	To create an attitude of mind which can match sensible controls with flexibility	?	✗
	HR managers	Create and manage reward processes that positively encourage innovation	✓	To study methods in use in other organisations in order to apply in our company	✓	✓
5 Culture of innovation with all staff	All staff	Positive attitude to 'newness'	✗	To explore creative thinking and methods	✓	✓
	People managers	Encouragement/support re ideas	✗	Enable managers to stimulate and manage ideas and experimentation	✓	✓

Values and beliefs in people development

This is the second 'general drivers' box on our model. What we do in HRD must support and be aligned with the values and beliefs that the organisation holds – as articulated by senior management or as generally accepted to be the 'way we do things'. Increasingly, organisations find it worth while to state deliberately and specifically what they believe about people development.

The 'psychological contract'

Much debate has raged over recent years about the changing nature of the 'psychological (that is, unwritten) contract' between organisations and employees. The old model is characterised by stability, mutual loyalty, lifetime employment if desired, managed careers, and pensions based on assumptions of long service. Competitive forces and globalisation have made this approach inconsistent with the flexibility needed in resource management, and so new terms like 'employability', 'multiple careers', and 'personal ownership of development' have arisen. Wendy Hirsh of the Institute of Employment Studies has drawn up a helpful continuum of the options that may be offered – see Figure 5, opposite.

At the left end of this spectrum, the fully managed career exists. Today this is likely to be confined to 'high potentials' and perhaps to 'new' graduates in the first two to three years. It is doubtful how much it was ever true for other groups, although many had the feeling that progression was continuous, helped by complex grading schemes and career structures. At the right end we have 'You are fortunate to have a job and you will be trained to do it well, and no more should be expected.' A few large companies have adopted this approach, but they seem rare; some smaller companies have always been like that, but even they are probably a minority. Most employees fall into the middle area, where the issue is one of partnership and dialogue, of shared common interests, and where prime ownership of development generally lies with the individual.

Figure 5

OPTIONS FOR CAREER MANAGEMENT AND DEVELOPMENT

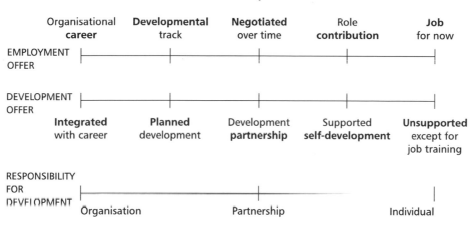

The career development continuum

Source: Institute of Employment Studies

Although the same principles should apply to everyone, in practice the 'contract' will be different for different groups, and it is as well to be open about this and to decide which processes will be put in place to support a) individual development, b) organisational talent growth, and c) dialogue between company and individuals. These are discussed further in Chapter 4.

> Draw up a list of the key subgroupings of people in your organisation who have common development needs (an example of such grouping is shown in Table 6). Where would you place each on the continuum of Figure 5?

Making decisions about our values and beliefs

Frequently sets of company values do not specifically include, surprisingly, anything related to learning or development! It is as if 'training' is accepted as something that one has to do, without seeing its significance in actually facilitating or accelerating progress towards business goals. To find corporate statements of belief in any more detail than paragraphs containing commitments 'to develop people to their full potential', or something similar, is quite rare.

A clear statement of beliefs will seriously aid an HRDM in creating an appropriate strategy. There are a number of options that can be expressed as a polarised scale – from a minimalist approach on the one hand to a dedicated learning organisation culture on the other. Few senior teams have sat down to consider what they believe is right for their organisation, although their decisions and priorities in fact show where they stand, and employees have their own perceptions of what they think top management believes. Porras and Collins, in *Built to Last*, referred to earlier, found the following:

- Long-lasting companies develop and promote insiders in preference to hiring outsiders.
- A high-profile charismatic leader is not required to create and run visionary companies.
- Clear, unequivocal cultural beliefs symbolise continued success.

Some of the options are encapsulated in a simple scale instrument in Table 7. It gives rise to these questions:

- Do we regard people fundamentally as costs, or do we see them equally as assets?
- Are we interested only in investing in those with potential for senior management, or do we recognise potential in everybody?
- Do we focus on the minimum training necessary, or do we see continuous learning as a way of life?
- Do we always seek qualified people who have been trained elsewhere or invest in accreditation for our own people?

Table 7

STRATEGIC OPTIONS FOR ORGANISATIONS IN LEARNING AND DEVELOPMENT

Place an asterisk for the desired position (the one you feel would be best for your organisation) and an 'o' for the actual situation today. Join up the asterisks and the o's. Which are the biggest gaps?

We act mostly on the basis that people are costs	We act mostly on the basis that people are assets
We are only interested in investing in high potentials	We believe in investing in the growth of all our employees
We only do training when essential	We believe continuous learning is a way of life
We hire people already qualified for vacancies we have	We help our employees with accreditation and employability
Managers decide what training is needed	We want all employees to take prime ownership of their development
People must look after their own careers	We believe in balancing the interests of organisation and individuals in managing careers
We budget for the training we can afford	Investing in people is a key competitive benchmark
We believe it is dangerous to give people views on their potential	It is better to be open and honest about development and have regular two-way dialogues
The training department is best outsourced	The learning support department is one of strategic importance
Co-operation with government initiatives is basically a waste of time and money	We value publicity from a reputation as an employer who cares about development

▌ Do managers decide what training is needed, or do individuals take primary ownership of their own development needs?

▌ Do we expect people to look after their own careers or acknowledge the need for balancing individual and organisational interests in career management?

▌ Is training budgeted as a cost to be minimised or at a level that reflects its competitive importance?

▌ Do we believe it is better to be open or cautious about discussing views of potential with people?

▌ Do we believe that training and development expertise should be outsourced or that it is of strategic importance?

▌ Do we see value in co-operating with government initiatives and having a reputation as a 'caring' employer?

Do we regard people fundamentally as costs, or do we see them equally as assets?

'People are our most important asset' is a common enough statement, yet frequently lacks credibility because the people themselves see what comes first in priorities. The preoccupation with headcount that prevails in many organisations is driven by a cost mentality, even though it is a very crude measure of human resource expenditure. People *are* costs, of course, and that cannot be ignored. However, unlike costs that are mere consumption, investment in them can increase their contribution and liberate potential.

Table 8 shows that not all human assets have the same value. Each organisation in its own market can evaluate where its employees fit into these boxes, and clearly the top right-hand quarter represents the highest asset value. Losing somebody in this category should be considered as disastrous and expensive as losing a key customer.

Table 8

HUMAN ASSETS

Difficult to replace Low added value	Difficult to replace High added value
Easy to replace Low added value	Easy to replace High added value

> Think of some categories of staff in your organisation that would fit into each quartile of a chart like Table 8. How does this relate to normal ways of monitoring staff losses, and would it be helpful to change that? What do you estimate to be the cost of replacing individuals in the upper-right quartile?

If the organisation has an 'asset' mentality, it will want to:

∎ ensure that employees are helped to regularly assess their potential

∎ ensure that employees are focusing on continual learning and development

∎ be concerned that it understands the talent it has, and utilise and grow it effectively.

A 'costs' mentality treats people as mere human *resources*, to be used for as long as they remain useful. No investment is made in processes that are concerned with longer-term growth. People are bought and disposed of as needed.

When faced with the choice, most managements would aver that they recognise the asset value of people. The test comes when a short- or medium-term financial hurdle has to be crossed. My own experience as an HR director in situations where downsizing was needed was that a little patience and some dedicated redeployment effort more often than not took care of keeping the assets as well as saving the cash drain of redundancy. Alas, few managers are bonused on cashflow!

> List some recent decisions in your organisation regarding the deployment and development of people. Do they indicate more of a 'costs' mentality or an 'assets' mentality?

Are we only interested in investing in those with potential for senior management, or do we recognise potential in everybody?

Organisations have tended to distinguish between training functions that cover all staff and those that cover management – and then to give special attention to management development. A wealth of assessment technology has been devoted to assessing potential for senior management, together with bibles of global leadership competences. Of course, future senior management is a legitimate and serious concern – but this effort goes into at most 1 per cent or less of the available people. (They are perhaps best equipped to manage their own development anyway.) An alternative approach is this kind of statement:

> We believe everyone in this organisation has potential to grow, and will make available the same systems and processes for people development to all. However, individuals will follow different development paths and some will require more help from the organisation than others.

Following this line, we would provide tools and help for everyone to explore their potential, whether as management, technologist or other person with special skills. Organisations need world-class specialists in their core competency areas just as much as capable managers.

Do we focus on the minimum training necessary, or do we see continuous learning as a way of life?

Training may be given, but only when it is essential – required in order to operate the business, or, for example, to take advantage of new equipment or to implement a new government directive. At this end of the spectrum it is totally tactical. On the other hand, what might be called a learning organisation regards learning as continuous; both within and outside of the work situation. Instead of asking HRD to mount occasional or just in time events, it asks the department to create and maintain processes that ensure learning is being maximised all the time.

Do we always seek qualified people who have been trained elsewhere or invest in providing accreditation for our own people?

There is, on the face of it, quite a lot of financial sense in letting other people do the training necessary for qualifications. For this reason, some organisations refuse to hire new graduates but look for those with two to four years' work experience. The alternative view is that loyalty and cultural empathy is created by 'growing your own'. Furthermore, the image of an attractive employer is enhanced by providing opportunities to gain initial or further qualifications. Whatever approach is taken will determine the organisation's strategy for education.

Do managers decide what training is needed or do individuals take primary ownership for their own development needs?

The traditional organisation is one of hierarchy, where the 'father' and 'grandfather' approach is applied to the management of people. Because the managerial role is one of organising work and gaining results, it is naturally assumed that the 'boss' is the key person to advise on training, development or careers. The evidence is clear, however, that few managers do this well, despite training in feedback and coaching skills. Their priorities are with the tasks in hand. Many organisations persist in emphasising this managerial role, even going so far as to say the *primary* role that managers should have today is that of 'coach'. This is, in reality, rare – especially in middle and junior management, where the demands placed on them do not permit such a focus.

An alternative approach is to put the individual in the driving seat, and to give him/her the skills of needs diagnosis, of choosing a learning solution and of making sure it happens. Naturally, the manager is not removed from the scene, but the role becomes a supportive rather than a controlling one.

Where the organisation stands on this particular spectrum will have a profound effect on the HR department. If it is more towards the personal-ownership end of the spectrum, it will be investing more time in coaching individuals to take care of their own needs and less on reinforcing management's role.

Do we expect people to look after their own careers or acknowledge the need for balancing individual and organisational interests in career management?

It is popular to repeat the rhetoric that people should look after their own careers, and indeed they should. But if this excludes any interest in the talent and succession needs that an organisation has for its own benefit, then the business interest is certainly not being served. The guarantees of the past, and the corresponding complacency, may have largely gone, but continuity of relationships that bring mutual benefit is bound to be beneficial.

Is training budgeted as a cost to be minimised or at a level that reflects its competitive importance?

> Budgeting is often a strange art in organisations – a game to be played. Most budgeting systems fail to distinguish between expenditure that is actually an investment and that which is a straight cost of doing business. 'Training' is likely to be a cost line of its own, subject to rules regulating what may be included and what not. It will always be an imperfect measure of overall learning.
>
> If our mentality is 'assets'-oriented, we shall want to benchmark investment in people just as much as investment in product or service development. The alternative sees training as a discretionary spend, a candidate for cutbacks when times are hard, despite a budget that may be unspent.
>
> What would we include in the 'investment' category? Not training that *has* to be done to keep the business going. However, spending on education, on potential development for the longer term, in supporting change and culture-building...these all have a future pay-off and could be justified as investment.
>
> This is clearly a matter of some importance to the HRDM, who should be clearly aware of how much activity and spend is in the two categories. Indeed, HRD might want to influence the thinking of top management regarding 'asset' investment. It will help considerably to have collected competitive data through benchmarking.

Do we believe it is better to be open or cautious when discussing views of potential with people?

> Many appraisal systems have a part for potential assessment that is never seen by the employee concerned. Some people are never told the extent to which they are, or are not, deemed capable of going further in the organisation. The arguments for the alternative approaches are:

Closed	**Open**
▌ Most people have a higher opinion of their potential than is deserved.	▌ People are not stupid. It is a myth that everyone is ambitious.
▌ It is unwise to provide people with expectations that may not be met.	▌ Good people will leave if they have no dialogue about their future. The fact is, potential is a perception at a point in time, and may change. Discussion helps to position expectations realistically.
▌ Since so much judgement is involved, you cannot be accurate and objective, and yet people will think you are.	▌ It is better to share opinions about people with them, and to have mutual discussion.
▌ Succession-planning is a management task.	▌ Career development is a mutual task.

The arguments for being secretive carry little or no weight in an organisation where we want people involved in their own development. Even outside that, they are hard to justify because they lead to misunderstandings and demotivation.

Do we believe that training and development expertise should be outsourced or that it is of critical strategic importance?

Any specialist support function is a candidate for outsourcing. However, many organisations have regretted doing this with specialist or administrative functions because the people involved lose their commitment to the parent organisation. If people development is truly seen as strategic, it is unlikely that the role of the HRDM would be taken over and key decisions about priorities would be made externally. External *help* may be utilised, but the ownership would be firmly anchored internally.

Do we see value in co-operating with government initiatives and having a reputation as a 'caring' employer?

All governments create initiatives designed to encourage training and qualifications, to reduce unemployment, and to grow the nation's skills. Some defeat their aims by persisting with stultifying bureaucracy, which is anathema to employers. Organisations take different views about social responsibility in this area. One of the best accepted in recent years in the UK has been the Investors in People (IIP) standard, perhaps because of its constant promotion as a benefit to any business. Once the standard is achieved, companies of all sizes are proud to display their shield prominently. Others take the view that they do not need to be assessed by outsiders in order to be told whether they know what they are doing in relation to their people and their development needs.

The HRDM may be involved in making the case for or against involvement, and certainly will be taking on most of the work involved in many such initiatives.

> Do the exercise in Table 8 for the organisation you are part of. Are there any areas in which you think that top management's might differ from your own judgement? How could you check that out?

The learning organisation: a few words

Taken as a whole, the right-hand statements of Table 8 could be said to describe some of the characteristics of a learning organisation, to which many HRDMs will be personally committed. What is it that makes the difference, given that all organisations do learn daily? The answer lies in the deliberate management of learning processes. The distinctions were articulated by consultant and writer Bob Garratt:

- Learning organisations encourage people at all levels of the organisation to learn regularly and rigorously from their work.
- They have systems for capturing learning and moving it where it is needed.
- They value learning, and are able to continuously transform themselves.

The term does not often excite senior management because it inevitably sounds like jargon. However, it can be pictured as a unifying concept for a culture of innovation, responsiveness, flexibility and change – and these are on the agenda of all managers. Managing learning effectively is very much about the efficiency of present performance, as well as growing knowledge and future value.

This implies a very different mindset from that of the traditional training department. It is about learning permeating the organisation's culture, and about a widely distributed ownership of continuous learning. Power is diffused from the training department as it becomes more consultative than controlling. Emphasis is placed on the process of learning rather than preprogrammed activities, even though such activities continue to serve a purpose.

A learning organisation is not just about good learning practice. It requires a supporting culture that *thinks* learning and values it seriously. Building such a culture requires a template, a description of the desired state against which progress can be measured. This requires some 'visioning' – describing 'what it would be like if this was a true learning organisation'. A framework such as that described by Burgoyne, Pedler and Boydell in *The Learning Company* (Maidenhead, McGraw-Hill, 1996) or by Mayo and Lank in *The Power of Learning* (London, IPD, 1994) can assist here. They have used models that define the contributing factors to a learning organisation (the latter based broadly on the popular European Business Excellence model), and posed questions that help teams to assess where they are and where they might like to be.

One key component of a learning organisation is its ability to *share* knowledge, learning and experience. This is facilitated by the use of IT systems, but depends essentially on human and cultural issues around the ownership of knowledge. In today's knowledge economy, senior management must seriously decide how it wants to manage this precious asset. Organisations are investing in positions such as 'chief knowledge officer' to give some coherence and discipline to the generation, capture, and distribution of knowledge across all organisational boundaries.

> List 20 characteristics that would describe your organisation if it were a 'learning organisation'. How does it rate today on a scale of 1 to 10 on each? Which three to five areas would really benefit it if tackled deliberately as a change project over the coming year or two?

> Who in management sees it as part of his or her responsibility to manage the sharing of knowledge and experience? List any gaps and inefficiencies in this vital process and suggest some ways forward – such as who should be influenced, what systems and resources should be put in place, etc.

Publicising statements of beliefs

As noted, it is immensely helpful to HRDMs to have an agreed 'charter' as a guide for their activity. If such a thing does not exist, should the HRDM then just do his or her best or actually seek such a statement? Many would compose one themselves and submit it to top management for their approval (and probably get it). It will be more powerful, however, if top management can define it in their own words – and preferably jointly as a team. Several solidly business-based reasons can be given for asking a top team to do this – not least to guide the HRDM to spend their resources 'strategically'.

We saw at the end of Chapter 2 a number of examples of corporate statements of one kind or another, many of which declared beliefs in some way. An example of a free-standing statement is that of Hertfordshire County Council, called their 'Development Charter'. This appears in full as an Appendix at the back of this book (page 196).

Often the beliefs behind people development are visible to employees through the processes that support it and through the documentation that they receive. Thus BT launched a 'Partnership' in career development and has a series of interlinked strands with their accompanying booklets explaining them. ICL produced three booklets in a series 'Investing in People' – covering performance management, managing learning and managing careers – that made clear the company's belief in the involvement of individuals in the three areas.

> List all the various documents available to managers and employees in your organisation that relate to people development. Note all the statements that they contain that are 'beliefs' or 'values' related to development. How happy are you with what you have, or to what extent could you envisage a more coherent statement of beliefs that would be helpful to all?

The third of the 'general drivers' – core competences

The third of the general drivers is that of the core competences of the organisation. This is not the same as the values, which are generally aspirational. By 'core' we mean the fundamental expertise that enables the organisation to be in, and stay in, its field. Hopefully, there are also some areas that distinguish a particular organisation positively from its competition, although these are not always so easy to find. It is these distinctive ones that make the difference, and if not clear it may be well worth choosing some to build.

As an example, Eli Lilly & Company, the international pharmaceutical company, has identified six 'core capabilities':

- innovation
- disease prevention and its management

- biotechnology
- speed to market
- information technology
- pre-eminent organisational effectiveness.

This is a mixture of 'capabilities necessary for the industry we are in' and 'areas in which we seek competitive differentiation'. A 'core capability' means that knowledge in it is continually updated, excellence is maintained, and all in the organisation who are affected will be evaluated for their expertise in it. The overall agenda for HRD must include continuous learning in the identified capabilities. In practice, the department may not actually manage many of the training courses and seminars, certainly of a technical nature, but it will be concerned to ensure that they take place and are effective. Outsourcing these areas is likely to be inappropriate because the organisation itself should have superior expertise as well as competitive advantage.

> What are the core competences of your organisation? Are they generally explicit? What in your training portfolio is designed to support them?

It is common today to identify behavioural skills that are core, in addition to business, professional or technical know-how. These may be those identified to support the corporate values and be applicable to every employee. (As Richard Boyatsis of Case Western University observes, 'Competencies without values is like sex without love.') Or, more commonly, they may be the desired characteristics of management or leaders. As such, they will be chosen as those that will generate excellence and advantage for the particular business – although competitors often have very similar sets! HRD will be expected not only to help individuals assess their capability but also to develop it. Table 9 on page 70 shows two examples.

Table 9

EXAMPLES OF CORPORATE-WIDE CORE BEHAVIOURAL COMPETENCES

BP Oil	Automobile Association
Leadership	*Senior management*
Respected player	Creates vision, strategy and direction
Leads change	Achieves excellent results
Strategic influencer	Lives the AA's values
Builds best team	Excels in influencing others
Shapes performance	Is great to work for
Strategic conceptualiser	Makes teamworking happen
Environmentally astute	Can develop an appropriate culture for the organisation
Ensures alignment	Is managerially and personally efficient

The 'specific' drivers of strategy

We have spent some time considering the 'general' drivers of strategy, which provide the umbrella for our activities but also have to be continually supported through learning. 'Specific' drivers derive from current business goals and plans. They differ from year to year and require responses within different timescales. What we have called 'proactive' endeavours are essentially about achieving future goals. Managers have a range of objectives for the year: some are about achieving the current quantitative goals; others are about new initiatives or plans for change and improvement.

Our model has four kinds of proactive drivers:

∎ business strategies
∎ business goals
∎ organisation and manpower plans

▌ change initiatives.

The business strategies and business goals

Goals, targets, objectives are typically financial, market-related, growth-related, even cultural or – occasionally – people-related. We may interact with them at corporate, divisional, departmental or individual levels. The question for the HR department is where and how it should make connections to these goals in order to apply methodologies such as the 'eight steps' described on pages 45–50.

Many will be interdependent, so it may not be necessary to take every goal individually but to see them as part of a whole. We may not have the time and resources to systematically apply our consultant method universally, and so we may need to seek guidance from managers on what the priorities are and which will have the most impact on people capability.

The business strategies are sometimes hard to find, especially if the so-called strategic plan is mainly financial figures. Such plans are extrapolations of history, devised with the aim of continuous growth propelling them. Our eight-step method can be applied to them, but sooner or later the question 'How?' will arise – and this can only be answered by strategic choices.

Some strategies have a specifically people-related component. Zeneca, referred to at the end of the last chapter, has a specific objective 'to ensure a well-motivated organisation in which people are respected, enjoy their jobs and obtain fulfilment'.

Such statements play directly into the 'beliefs about people development' that were discussed earlier.

Organisational and manpower plans

Organisational change may be a phased long-term plan, but more often is a series of projects that consume an immense amount of time and energy. One most likely impetus for restructuring is a change of CEO – newly appointed or as the result of a merger, for example. For some it seems to be the first thought on their agenda – not 'Should I reorganise?' but 'How shall I do it?' The top team may be advised by consultants that they would be more successful with a new model; and mergers and alliances almost always result in organisational upheaval. Market and technology changes force organisational change; and in recent years cost pressures have resulted in widespread de-layering and 'rightsizing'. It is positive to be flexible and adaptive – however, the cost of broken teams, relationships and new learning curves is rarely taken into account in the justifications for change.

Traditional organisation-planning focuses first on the positions to be filled and then on the people to fill them. Occasionally, it starts the other way round: how can we use the talent we have? The former forces greater learning – although a combination of both approaches makes most sense.

When it happens, it immediately triggers questions in the mind of the HRDM, who indeed should be involved preferably at the planning stage. These would include such questions as the following:

▌ *Does this change require a significant capability shift for groups of people to make it successful?* An example is a shift to a matrix organisation. It is more often than not *after* the event that we find out that people do not know how to work in such an environment; that they do not understand the cultures involved in their new responsibilities, or the market needs. Time and again multinationals give home-based managers responsibility for countries about which they know nothing. HRD should be experienced enough to discuss the competences needed objectively and check who has a learning need. People are sadly too impatient to get on with the new roles and, in so doing, cost their organisation unnecessary pain and money.

▮ *Does this change require significant learning curves for certain individuals?* Taking out layers in an organisation inevitably increases the accountability of the people below the vanished rank. Especially if relatively senior, they may be reluctant to admit that they are in new waters, and prefer to learn as they go. This is rarely efficient and can be costly. HRD needs to adopt a counselling mode, with knowledge of the requirements of the roles, and the ability to help the person assess his or her capability realistically. Another example would be international appointments – where ignorance of managing in different cultures can prove disastrous.

▮ *Does the change set up new boundaries and render obsolete existing mechanisms for exchange of knowledge and networking?* How will knowledge be managed and transferred freely in the new structure? Will new systems and networking opportunities be needed? This should be a part of planning and an area of expertise in which HRD can advise.

> List some problems you are aware of from recent reorganisations and try to cost those problems, if only approximately. How could more 'people capability planning' beforehand have prevented the problems, and at what cost?

Manpower planning is often neglected in the turbulence of corporate change, and some may feel it has little point to it. It is not the same as headcount control, which is a convenient and crude, if flawed, means of controlling people costs. It does include determining the *numbers* and *capability* of staff needed, but analysing manpower *flows* is also a vital guide to the planning of strategic *development*.

The business plan drives a set of numbers, including – let's say – a 'people inventory plan'. One reason headcount alone is unhelpful is that it assumes an average level of capability and contribution from each 'head'. The plan should detail the numbers of employees of different skills levels needed to deliver the financial market share and service-level goals. These numbers may be determined in various ways:

■ *by deriving an affordable headcount number from financial planning* – This is a very rough and ready calculator, and takes no account of the different costs and added value from different groups and skill levels. It is quite inadequate for strategic capability planning.

■ *job category/skill numbers by productivity* – More sophisticated, this takes into account differing productivity levels and works by improving productivity from its existing level rather than from just a cost parameter.

■ *ratio planning* – For indirect categories not connected with a front-line delivery, this is similar to the former method, by relating support levels to numbers of front-line staff.

■ *zero-based budgeting* – Starting from an imaginary 'greenfield', what would we need, given no history? This method involves benchmarking 'best practice', and is always useful to do. It rarely gives all the answers on its own because organisations always start with current reality.

■ *process re-engineering* – This is similar to the zero base, but examines all the processes for inefficiencies and improvements *first*.

■ *'added value' analysis* – This looks at where and how much added value is being added to the organisation's goals by each function *in cost terms*, and ensures resources are being utilised in the high-added-value areas.

■ *competency planning* – This is about having the right people with the right skills at the right time. Taking the average *numbers* per staff category, this then breaks them down into competency levels needed. Not every individual has to have the same level.

The outputs will be of great interest to HRD. One clear goal they have is to close the gap for each staff category between

$$\text{required } (Q \times Cn) \quad \text{and} \quad \text{current } (Q \times Cn)$$

where Q = number of people, and Cn = competence at level n.

Software can be created which looks at each individual (A=Actual level of expertise; R = Required level of expertise; R-A = the gap to be filled):

Specific competences →									
	A	R	R-A	A	R	R-A	A	R	R-A
Names ↓									

Manpower flow analysis is essential to show us the adequacy or inadequacy of *future* resourcing. It takes time to develop people. Have we the raw material to grow the managerial responsibility and technical/professional leadership we need to maintain our competitive position and/or meet our growth plans?

Our analysis would include the following:

■ mapping demographics, by function, division, location, staff category, etc.

■ tracing losses by staff category, and reasons for losses (the most common reason is lack of career or development challenge)

■ mapping patterns of career movement – average time in post, typical career 'bridges' between functions and locations

■ mapping the distribution of potential

■ relating the above to the growth plans of the organisation

■ mapping competency distributions within staff groups, as desired at points in the future and compared with today.

These analyses can yield a number of outcomes:

■ forecasting future flows out from, into, and within the organisation

■ consequent decisions about young-entrant recruitment, actions to reduce attrition in some areas

■ planning accelerated development for some individuals

■ strengthening of areas that are weak in potential and succession

■ taking action on retention of key and potential staff

■ creating new career paths

■ planning significant capability shifts (and preparing for them).

These outcomes will guide plans and activities for development, and may require some education or training solutions for their achievement.

> What analyses are done in your organisation? How often, and by whom? How is HRD involved?

Guiding Principle 6

We cannot plan sensibly for the development of
key resources for the future without intelligent
and analytical manpower-flow analysis.

Young-entrant recruitment is a particularly important area
for strategic decisions. It is amazing how short-term
organisations are here – deciding how many *they can afford*
each year. It is not as if the costs are great. This is the
tyranny of headcount control. Young entrants, other than
those specifically recruited for a here-and-now job, are
joining with the future in mind. The number needed is a
projection of the resourcing need in five to twenty years'
time, taking account of losses en route, and for a particular
set of roles, both managerial and professional.
Organisations that take this seriously – such as the major
consultancies – not only plan their numbers carefully but
have a clarity about what they seek in the candidates.

Guiding Principle 7

There is no business logic in deciding how many
young entrants should be employed based on this
year's progress against budget, and even less
based on headcount targets. Investments in
people need decision parameters different from
mere expenditure.

Despite the immense growth of personnel information
systems, the majority of organisations still lack the data
with which to do these studies. Data that they had may
have been lost. How many HRD departments have
manpower planning as a part of their remit?

The fourth proactive driver: change initiatives

Today, change programmes are ubiquitous and often so numerous that they become a burden on management. Most managers are conscious of several in which they are expected to play their part, in addition to their main accountabilities. It may be quality- or customer-related, process engineering, organisational restructuring, new systems, supply chain efficiency, alliances – the list is extensive. Managing change is a key preoccupation, and a source of considerable revenue to 'change consultants'. The basic guidelines for being effective should by now be well understood. Unfortunately, applying them all in conditions of insecurity and turbulence proves more difficult. Change initiatives invariably require training support, both in managing the process of change and in creating new levels of capability in individuals and teams.

The 'eight-step' methodology applies here equally well. Customised and often extensive programmes may be needed to ensure the success of major change initiatives.

> List the major change initiatives current in your organisation. When and how did HRD get involved in each implementation? Can you see ways in which a different level of involvement might help the initiatives?

Now for the reactive drivers

As opposed to proactive drivers, our model suggested four *reactive* drivers:

∎ operational issues
∎ individual needs
∎ team needs
∎ external changes.

Operational problems and issues

Here we mean practical operating problems in any part of the organisation – and every department has them – or shortfalls in performance goals.

Guiding Principle 8

It is likely that every problem in day-to-day life can be traced through to some inadequacy in capability – of employees, managers, leaders or teamworking. For HRD every problem is an opportunity – to see how effective learning can transform performance.

Again, the methodology described earlier can be applied. There is a need for HRD to always keep close to the business and its progress, and pick up signals as to where it might be able to help.

Being responsive to a cry for help comes naturally to most HRD departments, but being primarily proactive means constant tracking of the business. There may be a reluctance to be so because training plans have been set and resources organised and the flexibility to cope with new initiatives may not be there. Yet this could be a major way to add value.

Individual and team performance issues

The sister book in this series, *Identifying Training Needs* (T. Boydell and M. Leary, London, IPD, 1996), discusses three levels of performance and need:

■ *Level 1 Implementing* – doing things well
■ *Level 2 Improving* – doing things better
■ *Level 3 Innovating* – doing new and better things.

The first level is where there is a gap between the actual performance and the standard/desired/ targeted performance. It is primarily about maintaining basic requirements, and may involve both standard 'initial' as well as remedial training.

The second level is not just about individual improvement but the collective raising of standards. The third implies people who have sufficient mastery of the basics to begin to question and massage them in order to create new avenues. These three levels are additive and require different learning modes.

This is a helpful classification when we come to look at performance needs, because we risk being locked into the first level without perhaps realising the potential of the others. Thus, even when things appear to be going well, there is always a need to ask questions that relate to levels two and three. The classification also helps identify suitable learning objectives, modes and outcomes.

HRD will generally be keen to respond to requests to support group performance needs, although we should take care that we do not jump to the 'teambuilding' route to better performance. Most 'teambuilding' events are memorable experiences, either happy or traumatic ones, which leave their effect on the individuals concerned but *not* always on the performance of the organisation. That is because the goals are unclear and unspecific. Which triggers another Guiding Principle.

Guiding Principle 9

Any solution to team performance that is built essentially around the people themselves is dependent on the network of their continuing relationships. Where a team learns to set directions, agree goals, define procedures, measure and monitor performance together, then these have a better chance of lasting independently of the team members.

Generally, team training – where a group learns together – will be much more effective than occasional individual members' being trained from time to time. Where serious bottom-line performance improvement is needed, this is the route to effective investment.

Managing individual performance improvement is a more difficult area, because no HRD department can attend to the needs of hundreds or thousands of individual employees. Here we rely on a) processes of performance analysis (such as appraisals), and b) our philosophy of responsibility for individual development. Most organisations continue to emphasise the key role of managers being in taking responsibility for the development of their people, training them in coaching skills and so on. Others recognise that if the real ownership could be placed with the individual themselves, then – given comprehensive support – a greater degree of success in improvement is likely. HRD's role is to provide the processes and many of the supporting skills and resources – as well as to make the desired philosophy a cultural and everyday reality.

The world outside changes too

Our fourth reactive requirement is about demands placed on us from outside. In some sectors, external bodies demand training standards for all, and when these change, new initiatives are automatically required. These changes may be legislative, regulatory, or the result of social pressure. HRD has no choice but compliance, however occasionally irksome and unnecessary this may seem, and has to funnel the needs into the plans – the priority often being proscribed.

In brief

▌ We can distinguish between *general* and *specific* drivers of a business or public organisation. The former are semi-permanent and concerned with maintaining the organisation's main purpose and goals. The latter are about current strategies and plans. HRD has a key role to be linked to these, supporting them through learning.

▌ The *general* group includes mission, vision and value statements, and specifically the beliefs held about people development. These may not be explicitly stated, but it is very helpful to HRD (and to all employees) if they are. Also here are the core competences of the organisation, that distinguish it from other types of organisation and, hopefully, from competitors.

▌ This group also includes the *core competencies* of the organisation that need sustaining and growing.

▌ There are 'polarities' of approach to people development, and we can help management teams to examine where they feel they should be and where they are currently.

▌ HRD needs a systematic method for linking strategic and business goals with the learning process. In this chapter we described an eight-step method that can be applied to any of the drivers. The secret of business-linked training and development is to apply methodologies of this kind.

▌ The group of *reactive* drivers includes current business plans and goals, organisational and manpower plans, change initiatives, performance and operational problems, and external demands placed upon us. All of these need HRD support in some way.

Strategies for Professional HRD Management

If we have examined the drivers of strategy systematically, we shall have a series of potential learning goals. Before we motor ahead and turn them into plans, we need to think of the professional side of HRD and the choices it faces.

In this chapter we shall cover:

- HRD values and beliefs
- people development processes
- learning methodologies
- measuring and monitoring success.

Ideally, organisations articulate their beliefs about people development in an explicit way, as we described earlier. HRD's own beliefs and methodologies should be strongly shaped by the values and philosophy of the organisation itself, although sometimes the department strikes out on its own path, for better or worse. It may fill a void by designing and publishing documents that express its best understanding of the strategy the organisation wishes to pursue. The personal beliefs, experience and passions of the HRDM and/or his or her boss are bound to influence this. (Although we are being somewhat clinical in our systematic approach in this book, it is worth remembering how many passionate, even evangelistic, HRDMs have had a radical influence on their organisation.) In this chapter we want to consider the *internal* strategies that derive from the chosen beliefs and approaches in HRD, plus the systems and processes used to implement them.

What kind of mission, vision and value statements might HRD have?

The HRD department may want to have its own statements of this kind. A mission statement can be helpful if it forms a serious and meaningful guideline. Some examples of mission statements from various organisations are shown in Table 10.

Table 10

EXAMPLES OF HRD MISSION STATEMENTS

'ICL Learning only exists to help ICL companies to produce better business results. We achieve this, in partnership with our clients, by developing the crucial aspects of individual, team and organisational business capability to improve the performance of all our people at work.'

(ICL)

'To create a comprehensive and integrated process for continuous learning which enables the Company to achieve the goals of its Mission Statement, and enables employees to a) develop their potential, and b) make a direct contribution to the Company.'

(BAA)

'To develop the skills and encourage the release of the potential of all employees in order to deliver customer-driven continuous improvement.'

(Johnson & Johnson)

Vision statements that emphasise an overriding goal can be powerful. Examples might be:

■ 'HRD is a business partner at every level of the organisation.'

■ 'HRD adds at least three times more value than its cost.'

■ 'Our company is a true learning organisation.'

■ 'HRD is the recognised first source of help in all areas of employee development.'

In the British Airports Authority, the Training Vision was set in 1996 as:

> BAA will become a true Learning Organisation: our people will be the best in the industry world-wide and will be delighted by their personal growth and development during their career with the Company.

At a conference in the London Business School in 1998, a young manager from Hewlett Packard shared a 'vision' that a group to whom she belonged had created themselves as part of the support workshops provided them via HRD. It went as follows:

> HP is the best place to work for professionals and managers because we have learned to integrate our job and career with our life goals and values. We enjoy:
>
> personal fulfilment/enthusiasm/'resonance'
> loyalty of intellectual capital to HP
> higher-quality overall contribution to HP.

Somewhat detailed 'visions' are recommended for HRD embracing a range of medium- and long-term goals. When computer systems company ICL changed its training department to the 'ICL Learning Consultancy', its vision included statements about what it would be like in three years' time, covering the following:

- client profile
- turnover
- share of company training costs
- growth
- resource profile and utilisation
- client feedback
- average assignment length
- standards of operation
- internal commitment
- competitive competency levels.

The advantage of this comprehensive approach is that it readily leads to milestones against which progress can be measured.

Values for HRD departments

One key role of HRD is to support and bring alive the organisation's values.

Guiding Principle 10

Rather than create additional new values of its own, HRD should define behaviours that exemplify its own living of the corporate values.

Table 11 shows some typical examples:

Table 11

HRD BEHAVIOURS SUPPORTING TYPICAL ORGANISATIONAL VALUES

Value	Positive behaviours	Negative behaviours
Excellence	■ Professional quality of administration	■ Trainers not keeping to their objectives
	■ Highly positive event feedback	■ Lack of information
	■ Quality of materials	■ Sloppy, poorly prepared support materials
Customer focus	■ Trainees as customers – meeting their needs is the priority	■ The department's focus is on its own efficiency and convenience
	■ All events focus on/refer to external customers	■ External customers do not feature in most events

(continued on page 88)

Table 11 (continued)

HRD BEHAVIOURS SUPPORTING TYPICAL ORGANISATIONAL VALUES

Value	Positive behaviours	Negative behaviours
Self-development	■ Delegate feedback is taken seriously and responded to	■ Obtaining feedback is no more than a routine exercise
	■ Systems for training and development start from the principle of personal ownership by individual employees	■ Programmes are essentially trainer-driven
	■ Programmes always feature personal actions before, during, and after an event	■ Little or no resource is put into self-development centres or helping people evaluate their development needs
	■ HRD staff set an example through their continuous personal development	■ Systems and processes feature the manager as the prime decision-maker in people development
Achievement	■ The HRD function has a clear set of measures that are continually monitored	■ Poor performance is tolerated and not dealt with in the department
	■ Individual department members are stretched to perform	■ Activities themselves are more important than what they achieve
	■ Systems are in place to measure learning achievement	■ No interest is taken in the organisation's business goals and achievement

Internal strategies: basic beliefs and approaches

Table 12 shows a simple tool for evaluating strategic options for HRD, similar to the one shown in Table 7 for the overall organisation.

Table 12

STRATEGIC OPTIONS FOR PROFESSIONAL HRD

Place an asterisk for the desired position (the one you feel would be best for your organisation) and an 'o' for the actual situation today. Join up the asterisks and the o's. Which are the biggest gaps?

Our job is primarily to run good training events	Our job is primarily to facilitate learning in a variety of ways
On-the-job learning is the manager's task	A key role we have is to help everybody maximise the learning from everyday work
Pre-course and post-course activities are the responsibility of the line managers	It is our responsibility to ensure the learning process is complete
All training activity should be co-ordinated by us as professionals	We are happy if a variety of learning activities happens across the organisation
Our training needs analysis is based on our course schedule	We start with defining learning needs and develop solutions using a range of learning options
We accept whoever is sent to us	We always check the reason for choosing an event and suggest alternative learning approaches where relevant
We build into our schedule what we think is good for the organisation and its people	Our activities are prioritised according to the business needs, both current and future
Our focus is on individual and team learning	We work as much with organisational learning as with teams and individuals

> What values do you have in your organisation, and how does (could) HRD exemplify them in its activities?

Many practitioners will readily align themselves with the right-hand side of Table 12. The test is to coldly analyse where time and effort are actually being spent.

> Do the exercise in Table 12 for yourself (if working in HRD). Then ask other colleagues to do it according to how they see HRD operate. What lessons do you learn from any differences?

The exercise gives rise to consideration of the following topics:

- the focus on training *v* learning
- the manager's role in on-the-job development and coaching
- roles in the overall learning process
- the issue of ownership
- training schedules *v* customised learning solutions
- 'bums on seats' *v* learning effectiveness
- HRD's agenda *v* the organisation's needs
- individual, team and organisational needs.

The focus on training v learning

Although learning is the word on everyone's lips, in practice most HRD functions still have a heavy emphasis on the design and delivery of events – maybe using a variety of learning techniques within them. Training is a vital part of the overall learning process, and it is not a question of one or the other. However, it is recognised that maybe more than 80 per cent of our learning comes from experience and work itself, and at most 20 per cent from off-the-job events – yet the effort and attention devoted by HRD functions is generally the inverse of this. The spectrum represents two different mindsets. The one is event-, 'teacher-' and solution-centred; the other is process-, 'learner-' and problem-oriented. This fundamental belief will significantly affect the way HRD is directed, prioritised and measured. It will also affect the resources we need and their skills – see Chapter 6.

The manager's role in on-the-job development and coaching

In many organisations a tremendous effort has gone into providing managers with coaching skills in order to encourage their role in people development. At the same time, this has gone hand in hand with a general escalation in the pressures put on managers from all quarters. Although there are always role models, the reality is that only a minority of managers actually exhibit, or have the time to show, good coaching skills. However, if the individuals who have the learning needs can be helped to manage their own learning processes and be skilled at calling on support from their manager or team leader as necessary, then we have a different dynamic. The question therefore is how much effort to put into the skill improvement of both managers *and* staff in rigorous systematic learning from work experiences.

Guiding Principle 11

People development, including the use of coaching, will be more effective the more individuals are able to own their needs and manage their learning. Managers should support them and provide opportunities, but not be in control.

Roles in the overall learning process

The problem of most training events (especially in management) is that there is great diversity of individual need, of individual motivation and of the environment to which the learner returns. Managing training as a discrete event is inadequate – the 'end-to-end' learning process requires discussion about what needs to be learned beforehand and application of what has been learned afterwards. Nevertheless, sadly, very little pre- and post-activity takes place in most organisations. 'It is the manager's job', is the response, and some go so far as to say, 'We insist the relevant discussions take place.' The question here is whether HRD believes it has a role in managing the *overall* process of learning. It cannot monitor what happens with every individual piece of learning, of course, but it can create a system that enables each individual to maximise the learning possibilities.

The issue of ownership

Under the banner of 'quality control', some HRD functions will insist on control of everything that is to do with training. All kinds of reasons may be given why this would be of benefit. On the other hand, the HRD belief might be that the more distributed learning activities are, the more likely it is that a learning culture will develop. It sees its role as creating *competence* in others in respect of systematic learning processes – devolving its own expertise and acting in an advisory and consultative role. One can immediately see the effect of different beliefs here on what HRD does: a critical strategic decision.

Training schedules v *customised learning solutions*

Often there is an expectation from much of the organisation for a catalogue of training events, and it takes a long time to change this to an acceptance of custom-built solutions. The test is that a training event should be a conscious choice as the right mode of learning for the individual and his or her need at that time.

The appraisal system design can affect this considerably. Does it direct people towards a course solution? If it is derived from current or previous course catalogues, it perpetuates the *status quo* in terms of offerings. On the other hand, if the need is clearly defined, HRD or HRD-trained people can help choose an appropriate solution for the need. The former is much easier to manage from everyone's point of view... Unfortunately, it results in a lot of wasted training days when the wrong solution is matched to an ill-defined need. This issue radically influences the training needs analysis process.

'Bums-on-seats' v *learning effectiveness*

The pressures to fill advertised events may be significant – resource productivity, committed costs or target numbers This often leads to the cheerful acceptance of quite inappropriate event members. This is bad news for everybody – wasted days of training, frustration for tutors, for participants and for other delegates. The question for HRD is 'What are the criteria of success?' Are they driven by numbers or by measured learning achievement? It may be argued that it is impossible to check every event thoroughly for the latter. Once again, however, the answer probably lies in the *process* – in the questions asked and in the competence of individuals themselves in managing their learning.

HRD's agenda v *the organisation's needs*

Few HRDMs will say other than that they do their best to focus on the organisation's needs. However, in practice this may mean they decide, in best faith, what they believe is right for it. That belief is inevitably conditioned by where they come from personally. HRD has a significant share of idealist, relationship-oriented trainers who are quite lost when it comes to business issues, and who believe that the problem for their organisation is that it is *over*-task-oriented and insufficiently *people*-oriented. If our model for creating a strategy is followed, this should not be the case – but when setting priorities HRD needs to be very objective.

Individual, team and organisational needs

The learning-oriented HRDM will recognise the effectiveness of learning in teams and groups, and that, for significant behavioural change, people need to act according to shared values and mindsets. Time will be spent with business units to look at opportunities for team learning. This does not only mean team-building *per se*, which focuses on relationships and personality balance. As our ninth Guiding Principle reminded us, learning together about business-driven issues is probably the most effective route to team-building – the goal being something beyond just a 'better' team. With today's pace of organisational change, any benefits from most teambuilding exercises have a very limited life. However, decisions and change decided by a team may live on.

Organisational learning is about managing knowledge across the organisation, changing culture, and having an external focus. The HRDM may feel these issues are beyond his or her control and influence. It is also hard work compared to managing training events that people really enjoy. If we follow the logic of our model, it *must* lead into some areas that are about learning for the organisation as a whole.

> Looking at your current programme of events, what proportions would you classify as aimed at individual, team or organisational learning? How do you feel that reflects the business and strategic priorities?

People development processes

The beliefs we have discussed above will condition the methodologies used and the nature of the resources needed. The way the HRD department works clearly affects its efficiency, its resource requirements and its reputation. This is not the book to describe in detail the nuts and bolts of such systems and processes, but we do need to look at some of the choices that have to be made.

Should HRD be involved in strategic and business planning?

Every organisation does some kind of planning. The textbook model is a three- to five-year strategic plan, plus a one- to two-year operational plan and/or a one-year budget. There is a strong case for abandoning the constraints that the one-year budget brings, and there is a move to abandon such fixed periods. Table 1, on page 9, provides a hierarchy of involvement in strategy planning, and Chapter 7 looks at how strategic partnership can be increased. The questions for HRD are these:

■ At which levels, and how, should HRD be involved?
■ To what extent should capability planning be built into the process itself?

If we believe that training and development are a vital support for business goals, then something like the 'eight-step' method would be an integral part of planning.

The importance of capability frameworks

'Capabilities' (the word we shall use rather than 'competencies') provide bridges between personal assessment and job opportunities – they are the matching 'glue' between people and posts that enables objective comparisons to be drawn by both organisations and individuals, using a common language. Such processes include:

■ recruitment
■ selection
■ promotion
■ career-planning
■ continuity-planning
■ role descriptions
■ development-planning
■ performance assessment.

Behavioural capabilities alone are insufficient for such comparisons, of course: business, professional and technical competencies are critical for most of these comparative processes.

Learning objectives for individual (and team) development have to be based on some description of capabilities. The question is 'What *level* of capability are we aiming at?' The answer is often very vague, especially in the personal skills area – 'developing leadership skills', 'improving communication skills', 'providing diversity awareness', and so on. For this reason the link between the real learning need and a chosen training course (which has its own set of objectives) may be tenuous.

There are many models for describing capability, and a good one should meet the following:

▌ It should be *practical* to use by all employees and managers – not require specialist help to understand its complexity.

▌ It should be *useful* in making key processes work – a means to an end and not an end in itself.

▌ It should be *flexible* and adaptable, applicable to many different environments or situations – not a universal panacea.

▌ It should enable *distinctions* between levels of requirement to be made – but simply, and not requiring complex assessment procedures.

There are many models of competency available, and companies have invested heavily in their development. The author's consultancy practice uses the following model.

The components should be divided as follows:

▌ *personal skills* – characteristics relating to personality and behaviour

▌ *technical, professional and business know-how* – the core that drives output in the role

- *experience* – the specific situations experienced, their breadth, depth, problems and uniqueness
- *network* – the range of people needed to support a role, or on whom an individual can call for help.

The application of these are channelled through the *attitudes* and *values* that an individual holds.

Each identified capability should be supported by examples of how they are demonstrated at different levels of expertise. Joanna May of ICL developed a very simple but powerful level classification that for some capabilities may need no further expansion:

A = Aware, B = Basic, C = Competent, D = Distinguished,
E = Expert

These levels are essential in development-planning and setting learning objectives, so that we can be clear about the learning gap we are trying to close.

Positions – roles – are more helpfully described in these capability terms than as traditional job descriptions. Each role has three, cumulative, sections that add up to the capabilities required:

- core personal behaviours, attitudes and/or business knowledge expected of every employee in the organisation
- the set that is common to the job family to which they belong
- additional capabilities specific to the role.

All role descriptions should distinguish between the essential entry criteria and the learning opportunities that the role potentially brings.

As roles become more senior, and people become more experienced, 'experience' and 'network' play a greater significance both in the needs of a role, and in the value that a person may contribute.

Individuals should keep a personal *capability profile* constantly up to date, which summarises their distinctive capabilities in each of the components.

> If your organisation has a capability (or competency) framework, how and where is it used? How might you extend its application to new processes and new groups of employees?

Many organisations have moved towards competency-based pay systems, and HRD needs to be involved closely in all such initiatives to be sure that the messages employees receive are internally consistent.

The fundamental processes of performance and development review

The most significant means of identifying individual development needs is performance appraisal. The objectives of many systems are confused, and the development outcome may take second place to the determination of a pay decision. Two distinctly different processes are involved – one to assess *performance* against some expectations or targets; the other to look at capability, the strengths and weaknesses that lie behind the performance.

Some organisations separate the two physically and request two reviews. Others combine them. The HRDM would want to be sure that the *development* discussion is not being compromised or diluted in any way. He or she will also be concerned about the range of feedback involved in the process. The traditional manager-to-employee appraisal is fine for discussing achievements, but severely limited in its ability to cover the whole range of performance, especially the area of personal skills. The job itself is the richest source of learning, and therefore analysing and understanding performance is very important.

The people who see the true *how* of performance are other team members, subordinates, colleagues and customers (internal or external) – and much of what they see is hidden from the nominal boss. For development purposes, some form of 'multi-input' or 360-degree appraisal process has great benefit – and not just for managers. Anonymity is normally guaranteed, but HR departments can be oversensitive about the potential dangers of open one-to-one feedback. There is a good argument that people should be able to make their own choice of how feedback should be provided. My own personal experience of complete openness was immensely valuable.

HRD is usually looked to as the designer of appraisal and related processes. It is a fundamental platform in people development that makes a significant contribution to the dialogue between individuals and the organisation they work for. There are many aspects of their design that will give clear messages about the values of the organisation, and therefore deserve much thought. These include who is involved in them, how frequently they occur, who owns the outcome of them, how they interface with other processes, how much they reinforce the stated values of the organisation, their influence on selection for a future job, ratings and how they are used...and so on.

> What are the desired outcomes of your appraisal/ development processes? Are the development outcomes compromised or less than fully optimised in any way? How could you ensure that they contribute more effectively to the real development of the individual and to his or her performance?

The difference between training and learning plans

The detail in the design of a process that connects business goals with HRD is a very visible reflection of HRD priorities and beliefs. For a comprehensive study of training needs analysis, readers are referred to the companion volume in this series, *Identifying Training Needs* (T. Boydell and M. Leary, London, IPD, 1996). When it comes to individuals, the question is whether plans are driven by the solution-provider or by the learner. In a traditional appraisal model, at the end of the discussion the manager studied a list of training courses available and chose some for the appraisee to attend over the coming year. This choice was loosely based on the manager's personal perception of need, plus the appraisee's desire for what interested him or her. The training manager received copies of the appropriate page of the appraisal in order to formulate the demand for the catalogue they had already produced. The result was:

■ Learning solutions were conditioned by the types of course available.

■ Managers were often unskilled in the definition of learning objectives and chose courses for a variety of reasons ('You haven't been on this one yet'; 'This will make a nice change for you'; 'This looks about right for the problem we discussed'; etc).

■ Employees waited to be given the opportunity to attend.

■ Training was a programming activity, and self-perpetuating.

There is certainly a place for a catalogue of courses, particularly those concerned with know-how. But this approach produces an immense amount of wasted training days, and often fails to meet vital learning needs.

The personal development plan (PDP) has many advantages by comparison. This is not an integral part of an appraisal form to be filed away, but a live and current document owned by individuals themselves. A good design will focus attention on setting clear learning objectives, on choosing from a range of learning methodologies, and be prioritised according to practical realities. It should be designed to be owned by the individual, with management in a supporting role.

A PDP might have four separate inputs:

I   needs arising from *performance*, through the appraisal process or other work-based discussions

I   needs arising from potential *new requirements* in the current role; this requires a dialogue with management as to how the role will develop, need new knowledge or skills, or even disappear altogether

I   needs arising from *career aspirations*: these would be for capability enhancements which would not necessarily change the current role but which would help growth towards a target job

I   needs arising from *desires for personal development* unconnected to the other categories; the organisation's willingness to allow these will depend on the breadth of its overall beliefs in people development.

The way such plans are implemented will reflect the approach to personal ownership and self-management of learning. Implementation may be left in the hands of the manager to initiate as appropriate or with the individual. If the latter, some negotiation of time and money is needed before ownership can be real, as well as some training in the skills needed for self-management.

If self-management is chosen, the organisation may consider some computerised tools to help employees. For example, in organisations like Hewlett Packard and Sun Microsystems people can determine their own profiles and match them electronically against any job in the company. Furthermore, when a capability gap is identified that should be met by a training course, they can access the courses available and book themselves on what they want without leaving their screen.

Development and career management processes

The task in career management is threefold:

■ to understand the organisation's needs for future capability, and to know what talent it has available to it

■ to provide, as far as possible, a career challenge to individuals that helps them meet their aspirations

■ to provide means of dialogue between the two.

Table 13 illustrates the range of processes that we might draw from for these three areas – in addition to a capability framework that provides a foundation for most of them.

Table 13

PROCESSES FOR DEVELOPMENT

Individual support	Organisational interest	Dialogue
■ accreditation	■ organisational mapping	■ performance management
■ career-counselling	■ succession-planning	■ appraisal discussions
■ career-planning workshops	■ secondments	■ career discussions
■ personal development plans	■ manpower/skills planning	■ development centres
■ mentoring	■ training prioritisation	■ vacancy management
■ learning resource centres	■ retention strategies	■ self-managed learning
■ 360-degree feedback	■ potential assessment	■ managerial coaching
■ external coaching	■ high-flyer development	■ flexible working

Wendy Hirsh, while with the Institute of Employment Studies, also developed a summary of processes used in career development, which she categorised in five areas:

- assessment – how to determine development needs
- understanding available options
- job access – finding out about and accessing alternatives within the organisation
- skill development – growing personal capability
- planning and action – determining where an individual wants his or her career to progress, and taking relevant action.

HRD has to choose:

- which processes it needs to support its strategies
- how sophisticated those processes should be (culture, cost, ease of maintenance)
- who will own them
- what the respective roles of managers, individuals and HR/HRD will be in their implementation.

List the processes used in your organisation under the three headings of Table 13. How balanced are they? Do you feel there are some gaps to be closed?

Mapping the opportunities in an organisation

We noted on page 90 that upwards of 80 per cent of development comes through experience, work situations and taking actions ourselves. A manager and an employee can work together to maximise this from a current job. But what about *beyond* the job?

Organisational mapping is about understanding the opportunities that the organisation can provide in the big picture. It is about answering such questions as:

- What are the capability characteristics of different types of job in the organisation?
- Where can people get specialised experience such as staff-management, strategic thinking, project management, international, customer-facing, etc?

- What are the typically 'easy' boundary-crossing 'bridges' (for example, from manufacturing management to HR or from finance to strategic planning)?
- What positions do we have that could be classified as 'development posts' – ie an able individual could make a positive contribution to the role within three months without prior technical or professional know-how? (These should never be blocked.)
- Where do we have standing committees or require representatives on external bodies?
- When and where are we going to have some special projects, and what particular learning opportunities will they provide?

It is possible to computerise such a map to be available to all for navigation or career planning. But at the very least the HRDM should have it!

> If you do not already have the answers to these questions in your organisation, try obtaining them.

How do we decide to assess potential?

One of the key beliefs will be about potential: are we interested in everyone or just a few? If the former, we shall want to provide a means of assessment for every individual. Development centres, which help test against a preset number of capabilities together with feedback, are often used. These 'simulations with observation' have considerable face validity, but their very real danger is that the inevitably artificial performance situation is compounded with the often limited skill of observers to come to a conclusion that can be rather mechanical. Furthermore, it cannot be taken as having greater validity than what has been observed in real work situations. Organisations that believe strongly in mutual support in career management (such as Sun Microsystems, NatWest

Life, Hewlett Packard) combine an opportunity for assessment with a number of other dialogues and analytical tools about personal motivations and aspirations.

If, however, we are only interested in finding out who has senior management potential, we can rely more on the judgement of existing managers. This may be as unsophisticated as a boss's potential rating on an appraisal form, through a facilitated team review of all current managers, to comprehensive simulations and focused assessment centres. The latter are quite unnecessary for those who clearly have potential in the judgement of all. The professional added value of the HRDM is to choose an appropriate method in the circumstances – and this will relate to the extent of the track record available.

In this context, another strategic question is whether to be open or not about potential assessment and classifications. Shell (and others) utilise a very helpful classification under the title CPP – Current Perception of Potential. This recognition that any potential classification is only a perception at a point in time makes it much easier to have a dialogue around it. In choosing classifications, options available include:

▌ an assessment of *speed* of rising responsibility (eg two levels within four years)

▌ an assessment of *levels* beyond the current one (able to rise two levels)

▌ an estimate of the person's *ceiling* ('will make Grade 15').

The arguments for being open or otherwise were enumerated on pages 63–4 in Chapter 3.

If the capability framework is comprehensive and widely understood, then dialogue about the future is made much easier. We can focus on 'what it will take to reach your aspirations' rather than have an argument about perceptions.

Vacancy management: what access shall we give to opportunities?

Here there may be a dilemma between *open access* to jobs and *planned development,* where the two might be seen to be in conflict. It is a key policy decision as to which jobs will be openly advertised. In general in the public sector it is the norm for this to be done for all; practice in the private sector varies enormously. Some companies do so only when all else has failed; others make it a norm for all but the most senior posts. If an organisation is preaching personal career ownership, it seems inconsistent if people do not then have the opportunity to apply for jobs openly. The ability of managers to block applications from their staff has to be controlled too.

The advent of organisational intranets and web pages has encouraged the use of them for advertising internal vacancies, and this increases the availability of such information, especially across boundaries. Sun Microsystems, for example, advertises every job in the world (other than the three top levels) to every site, and anyone can make an application (electronically, of course).

Whatever is done has to have credibility and has to be more than a showcase behind which selection is fixed. The more 'shared' the information about aspirations and perceived potential, the easier it is to have coherence between the planned and the open.

What methods should we use for 'continuity' planning?

Most organisations need to develop their talent proactively and plan for succession, even though many are conscious that they do not do it well. Management looks to HRD to recommend the process to be used. Some of the design questions are:

∎ Do we want to identify successors for specific posts or create 'pools' of people available for similar types of positions?

∎ How far ahead do we want to look?

■ How shall we obtain and review the information?

■ Do we only want to look internally?

Do we want to identify successors for specific posts or create 'pools' of people available for similar types of position'?

Pools are more flexible, and provide a more reliable picture of succession strength. Organisations are generally focused on management when it comes to continuity-planning. However, the depth of specialist expertise and technical/ professional leadership is increasingly a major factor in competitive advantage. We need to ask whether we should have some way of assessing the growth of excellence in our core competencies.

How far ahead do we want to look?

One of the more useful 'markers' to apply to current incumbents is EDM, the Earliest Date for Move – that is, the earliest date at which the individual should be considered for his or her next career move. In continuity terms, we want to have a) an option for the unexpected, and b) an option ready at the time of the incumbent's EDM.

How shall we obtain and review the information?

Here there are a legion of options. HQ staff can tour the organisation asking the relevant people for their views. Local management teams can submit forms and papers. HR can manage it through their own hierarchy and network. Annual meetings can take place of continuity-planning subcommittees, resourced by an HR secretariat.

A number of companies (eg ICL, Tarmac, Bass, Pearl Assurance) have adopted an approach that integrates continuity discussions with operational business reviews. Generally termed the 'Organisational and Management Review' (OMR) or something similar, it synchronises a formal review of such issues as succession, key people development, strategic training issues and potential strength with the cycle of business reviews. Typically, this might take place every four months, being cascaded upwards through business units and subsidiary companies, eventually reaching the CEO. Each level in the cascade generates information that feeds into the next level.

One can see many advantages in this approach. It puts the ownership with line management; links business performance with people capability, recognises the dynamism of organisational and people development, and provides continually updated succession information. Action to close gaps or deal with problems can be taken regularly.

Do we only want to look internally?

A few organisations have tried to create a 'shadow succession plan'. That is, where people are not available inside the organisation, who is there outside who might be earmarked for hiring (or trying to hire), should the need arise? This cuts out considerable time from the search process.

A 'partner' search consultant who knows the organisation well is needed for this. It is not easy to do (although its merits are clear) and is probably only worth doing for a small number of key positions.

It is clearly not easy to talk to people about vacancies that do not exist, so a very detailed knowledge of a target market is needed.

Using secondments for development

Secondments are one of the most valuable forms of development, especially in 'flatter' organisations. Relatively low-risk to all parties, they provide the opportunity for new learning through real-life experiences. This has been the traditional route for international assignments, and many organisations have deployed them on a broader basis – to project teams, to new departments, or from line to staff posts and vice versa. Hertfordshire County Council is one organisation that, in an effort to counter fewer traditional career opportunities, introduced a 24-page booklet entitled *Guidelines for Effective Secondments, Job Swaps and Job Shadowing*.

Encouraging or facilitating secondments is a rewarding exercise in people development. It helps to take some central ownership for the process because, with the best will in the world, guarantees made at the beginning of secondment may prove difficult to keep by the originating party (who might have left or been reorganised). It is a sad waste of valuable experience to see returning expatriates with nowhere to go. HRD needs to be closely involved with the 'expatriate' department – and preferably responsible for it. This is one case where firm guidelines and disciplines are needed to help the process.

Do we want to encourage self-managed learning?

If it is a policy to encourage this – as is common today – considerable involvement by HRD is needed. It is not just a question of saying to people, 'Here is some money and here is a booklet to guide you.' Indeed, implementing such a policy would require significant resources for some time. People need to understand why it is in their interest, be motivated to spend time on themselves, and be trained in managing the processes of learning.

The process can be helped forward by setting up and facilitating 'self-managed learning groups'. Here, individuals interested in their own learning share their needs and progress, and use each other for help. The practical difficulties of self-managed learning can be shared and explored. Readers are referred to the companion volume (Megginson and Whitaker, 1997).

Do we need a systematic process for 'induction'?

Many firms are very casual and perfunctory about this – a one-day introduction for a new employee to his or her local site, perhaps, and often nothing for internal transfers.

Others take it very seriously: every new employee in Hewlett Packard must go through an off-site event that helps him or her understand 'what it takes to work in HP'. This covers corporate values, processes and policies. Relatively few organisations systematically organise induction for *internal* job changes. Often this is because so few of these changes are planned and there is always an urgency to get started. However, enormous productivity is lost as people sit on haphazard learning curves throughout the organisation. A significant hidden cost exists as a result.

A detailed example of a systematic, personalised, self-managed approach to induction is included in the author's book *Managing Careers: Strategies for organisations* (A. Mayo, London, IPD, 1992, pp298–301).

> What systems are in use in your organisation for both external and internal induction? What is their coverage in time and content? To what extent are they self-managed? In what ways do you feel that a more thorough approach would be beneficial to the organisation?

Professional methodologies in HRD work

We have already suggested some tools that might help to link business and learning. HRD does have to decide how it will collect and prioritise learning needs, and also what it will do with them – in other words, the professional design, delivery and evaluation of learning solutions.

This subject is covered in detail in companion *Training Essentials* books (see Further Reading). However, an overview might be helpful. What we might call 'end-to-end' solutions should be our goal. This means:

▌ we are confident that the learning need has been identified systematically

▌ it has been translated into specific learning objectives

■ we are able to design the learning solution that will most effectively achieve them

■ we are able to ensure that the application of the learning takes place and the need is a need no longer.

This takes us outside of formal HRD programming and into the concept of internal 'learning partnerships'. It involves working with managers and learners both before and after a formal event. In practice, this cannot be done with every course delegate, so a systematic process that enables the necessary steps to take place is needed. Help with setting learning objectives and with the choice of learning methods through booklets or questionnaires will be useful. ICL has a booklet for all staff called *Managing Your Learning*, BT has a *Development Options Guide* and BAA a *Guide to Learning* – all aimed at helping the individual manage learning beyond just training courses.

Application of learning back in the workplace is often left to chance, or the parting exhortation to 'discuss what you have learned with your manager'. Part of knowledge management is the transfer of knowledge and learning to others, and this is rarely evaluated. It should be an integral part of the overall learning design.

Guiding principle 12

Conducting 'evaluations' is about history. It does not guarantee the application of learning in the workplace, nor its transfer to others. This has to be planned for as part of the overall learning design.

Table 14 on page 112 provides some thoughts regarding application options for different types of need.

Table 14

SOURCES OF LEARNING AND MEANS OF APPLICATION

Type of learning	Sources	Means of transfer or application
New knowledge	Reading/other personal study Courses and programmes Seminars and conferences Personal discussion	Seminars, meetings Reports, summaries, papers Groupware, intranet Application to decisions and actions
New/enhanced skills	Coaching, imitation Training courses and programmes Experimentation	Changed performance and competence levels
Changed attitudes	Training courses and workshops Reading and personal study Influence of individuals Experience	Influencing others Application to actions and decisions Changed behaviour
New experience	Situations Projects Problem-solving Action learning	Presentations Reports, summaries, papers Groupware, intranet Application to actions and decisions
Increased network	Courses and programmes Seminars and conferences Use of internet Professional associates	Drawing on experience and best practice Ongoing sharing through meetings/internet

> Draw up a table like this for a selection of current HRD activities you are involved with.

Being an internal consultancy

If HRD wishes to position all or part of itself as an internal consultancy, the disciplines and routines of a consultancy need to be put in place. This will include:

- consultancy skills training
- a commercial structure
- time control disciplines
- utilisation targets
- project management
- resource allocation.

How will we know we are successful in HRD?

Success for HRD can be measured in a number of ways. Readers will probably be familiar with Kirkpatrick's levels of evaluation for training, ranging from event satisfaction to influencing the bottom-line results. There is some difficulty with this approach if the *starting-point* is the event itself. The starting-point should always be the learning objectives, defined before the event. (Readers are referred to the sister-volume in this series, *Evaluating Training*, P. Bramley, London, IPD, 1996.)

As we have emphasised earlier, it makes no sense to try to prove that every programme directly influences bottom-line measures. Too many factors are in play, and this may not have been the learning goal anyway.

Measuring HRD performance

'Happy sheets' filled in after events measure a part of customer satisfaction. Although they may not be a good measure of learning that has taken place, they give valuable feedback in their own right regarding the acceptability of material, trainers, environment, and so on. If this is the *only* measure of success used, we may have false illusions about what we are achieving.

Guiding Principle 13

To base an assessment of how successful we are on 'happy sheets' alone may mislead us significantly as to the value we are adding to the organisation.

The extent to which learning goals are met is the best measure. This implies that they were sufficiently well articulated in advance as to be measurable afterwards. There will never be a problem with evaluation if the objectives are clear. Goals should always include one or more of the following:

▌ a defined increase in capability

▌ a quantitative bottom-line measure – this may be a financial measure, a productivity measure (good for team development and leadership), a quality measure, or others, depending on the organisation

▌ a change in a survey result – perceptions of service, of management style, and so on (examples would be satisfaction surveys, 360-degree assessments and opinion surveys)

▌ the attainment of a qualification

▌ the building of a network

▌ experience of some particular situations.

Added value from, or return on investment of, HRD is a bottom-line measure. Not all HRD work is aimed at immediate bottom-line returns. Nevertheless, where it can be calculated, it is helpful to do so. One evaluates the full annual cost of the HRD function and its activities. Then for those events that are aimed at a change in a business result, estimate any annualised cost savings, productivity changes or the value of new revenues resulting from the training. This is then summarised and compared with the annual costs of running HRD.

HRD should be particularly aware of productivity measures in the different departments in the organisation – improvements would be expected from activities such as teambuilding (a notoriously unfocused activity in many organisations).

The business-minded HRDM will track certain costs that tend to be invisible in the accounting systems – such as the cost of replacing a key person who leaves the organisation or the cost of major errors arising from a lack of shared knowledge across the organisation. He or she would set targets for the percentage reduction of these costs, even though not directly under his or her control.

In development, we look for ratios that measure our success in the longer term, such as:

■ the percentage of positions with no successor coverage
■ the percentage of planned career moves that take place
■ the percentage of high-potential people by function/ division/area
■ the percentage of people with more than one year's international experience
■ the loss rate of high-potential people and other high-added-value personnel
■ the percentage of expatriates abroad for clear career development reasons
■ the ratio of executives in the top two or three levels who do not originate from the organisation's homebase
■ the percentage of people with the highest levels of the organisation's core competencies.

These can be divided up, of course, into relevant parts of the organisation, and this is recommended rather than averaging over the whole.

Internally within HRD, as for all well-managed functions, there will be standards of performance in relation to administration, response times and quality – which should be assessed by internal monitoring and occasional 'client' surveys. The distribution of competency levels in the function should be regularly compared with the ideal. Productivity of resources and utilisation of consultants will be measures, depending on the structure of the function. Other factors would include the ratio of support costs to direct costs, the utilisation of course availability, and so on.

> What measures are you using today? Who takes an interest in them? How complete are they in relation to the above? Would you see benefit in introducing some new ones?

Benchmarking

Benchmarking with other organisations is a valuable exercise, and can be done on a number of fronts:

▪ How do we compare in terms of our beliefs and philosophies?
▪ How do we compare in terms of efficiency?
▪ How well do we link our activities into the business priorities?
▪ How do we compare in terms of achievement of key goals?

Table 15 shows some questions for use in checking HRD efficiency.

Table 15

BENCHMARKING FOR HRD EFFICIENCY

Benchmarking questions

Questions can look at training and development for the whole population, or –
preferably – break the population down into such subgroups as: senior
management, middle/junior management, technical/professional, administrative
and support, operational, young entrants, etc.

1   What percentage of your training is managed centrally, as opposed to within
a local business unit?

2   What is the total absolute £ spend of running the central training function,
and what is this as a percentage of corporate revenue and paycost? (Exclude
delegate salary costs.)

3   What is the additional £ spend of locally run training events, both internally-
and externally sourced? As a percentage of local revenues and/or paycost?

4   How is budgeting for training done in your organisation?

5   What is the number of average off-the-job training days per person per year?

6   What percentage of a) training design and b) delivery is done i) by internal
staff and ii) by external resources?

7   What is the ratio of support staff to delivery staff in your training
department?

8   If you have central training premises, what is their cost as a percentage of the
total cost for central training?

9   What is a typical *per diem* charge for a delegate day a) with accommodation
and b) without accommodation?

10   What model do you follow for charging 'customer units' for the provision of
central training?

11   What is the estimated return on investment for your HRD function?

Some other questions might cover:

■ levels of involvement in strategy
■ methodologies for linking business goals to learning goals
■ the value placed on training as a support for business change
■ beliefs and principles
■ needs analysis processes
■ line-manager involvement
■ range of learning methods used
■ use of accreditation and management education
■ roles and skills in HRD staff
■ evaluation methods and results
■ organisational learning and knowledge management.

All benchmarking should have clear, focused objectives so that it does not result in masses of data that cannot lead to much action.

> Try these out for your own function. Are you happy that you are benchmarking enough and with the right questions?

In brief

■ There are some choices that HRD must make for itself. It has to determine its own approaches to how people develop, aligned with any explicit or implicit approaches that the organisation has. HRD may choose to have its own mission statement but, with respect to values, should support those of the organisation rather than create its own.

■ We can contrast approaches very broadly between those that are essentially *training*-oriented and those that are built to support a general *learning* culture. On page

89 a tool was described to help practitioners assess their functions.

∎ HRD has to design and maintain the systems and processes that involve others in people development. A systematic approach to describing capabilities (or competences) is fundamental to the management of learning processes.

∎ When we look specifically at development, there are three headings – those designed for individual support, those that meet the organisational interests, and those that are about dialogue between the two. HRD needs a balance between these.

∎ Companion volumes in this series deal with the professional methodologies of design, delivery and evaluation techniques, and these need to be chosen to complete the professional approach. (See Further Reading.)

∎ HRD is always vulnerable as an overhead and cost. It needs to have measures of its contribution and achievement, and these should include some assessment of whether learning has taken place as planned, and whether the added value and return from investment of HRD is positive.

∎ We always need to look outside as well as inside, so we need a benchmarking methodology that keeps us up to date with good practice elsewhere and enables us to see how we could improve.

5

Creating a Policy Framework

Policies are a practical expression of our beliefs. They provide guidance to managers and employees in deciding courses of action. They generally have *continuity*, and in this way differ from strategies that are about directional choices. Compared to general HR, there are a limited number of policy areas in HRD. However, they are less administrative and more strategic in their connection to the direction, values and beliefs of the organisation.

We look first at some of the strategic choices in policy formulation and then at some specific areas where policies are needed.

Strategic choices in policy formulation
How detailed and prescriptive should policies be?

Guiding Principle 14

Principles and beliefs should be universal – they should be formulated so that they are independent of local laws, customs and cultures. However, the practical application of those beliefs may, and often should, vary.

Organisations provide different degrees of freedom to their operations in how principles are applied. There is a spectrum that runs from 'We lay down principles only and leave interpretation to the units' to ' We research and define best practice in HQ and expect all our units to adopt it.' Many US organisations adopt the latter view and dictate procedures as well as the general policies; UK companies tend to do this less. Table 16 shows an example of decreasing degrees of freedom in the use of appraisal systems.

Table 16

DEGREES OF FREEDOM IN APPRAISAL SYSTEMS

It is a principle in our organisation that every employee should have a formal discussion regarding their performance and development regularly.

It is our policy that each unit should develop a performance appraisal system which is based on performance objectives, evaluates overall performance with a rating system, and discusses performance improvement and career development.

All local appraisal systems must utilise the global performance rating system, will appraise against the company's values and universal competency framework, and will be completed by the end of March annually.

All appraisals will conform to the corporate guidelines, and use Form XXXX, issue YY, translated as necessary to local language.

There is no right answer, of course: it depends on the kind of culture the organisation wants and on the issue. ICL, the computer company, re-evaluating its cultural framework after several mergers, in 1992 produced a booklet called *The Management Framework* that set out to lay down the minimum set of policies that would be universal. For HR there were 10, each described in one sentence, and in total there were about 30. This was a reaction to a formerly heavy hand from the centre, and also a genuine belief at that time that 'empowerment within policy and strategic guidelines' was a better way to manage and motivate people. (ABB, renowned for its devolved culture, has a booklet of *Global Values and Policies* with a much larger number of statements.)

One key question to ask is 'For whose benefit is the policy shaped?' If it is for the benefit of local employees, then the more localised the application, the more useful it will probably be. If, however, it is for the benefit of the organisation itself, then more consistency in application is needed. Another reason for commonality might be economics of administration, where to fund many different schemes would be unnecessarily costly. It is important to be sure that the expected benefits are being perceived locally when this is done. Examples of HRD policy areas are:

localised	globalised
Technical training	'Core competence' training
Education and qualifications	Graduate development
'Soft' skills training	Management development
Capability assessment	Succession planning
Trainee schemes	Potential classification

> What 'global' policies exist in your organisation? Who primarily benefits from them? Do you feel the balance between global and local is right?

Do we need special policies for particular staff groups?

Another dimension in application is its variation according to types of employee. Do we have differing appraisal systems for different groups? The modern tendency is for 'harmonisation', but it has been known for many schemes to exist within one operation – tailored to different employee and management groups. We noted earlier that it is helpful to divide the population into subgroups with common development profiles. For some groups our policy may be to provide more help than for others (eg career counselling or mentoring). Age may be another dividing line, as for example in policies on retirement planning or further education studies.

When we have mergers, acquisitions and alliances, how critical is it to move to common policies?

This an exciting area for HR and HRD, absorbing an immense amount of time and resources. There is a fundamental policy decision that is about a) convergence and b) its speed. Many companies exhibit an obsessive haste to create neatness out of disorder – common policies and approaches as soon as possible. Others value the diversity of experience that is available and seek to learn from it before creating compromise or imposing unilateral approaches.

There is much merit in taking the time to appreciate where talent, knowledge and wisdom lie in any new partner, and seeing that as a part of the relationship that is just as important as any financial or market share gain. HRD would expect to play a significant role in this. Synergy – a word that accountants have come to see as meaning potential cost cuts – should be about the fusion of intellectual capital and capability. What could be a more strategic role for the HRDM? Common appraisal systems can wait!

Specific areas where policies may be needed
What about the development of non-core staff?

Organisations today are far less homogeneous than before, when almost everybody was on a defined contract, either full-time or part-time, together with all the benefits of contractual employment. What Charles Handy has described as the 'shamrock' organisation is increasingly the pattern, where the core of contracted employees is complemented by temporary skills, regular contractors, interim managers, outsourcing partners, etc. Free of the liabilities associated with contracts, where does this leave employers in respect of development?

Again we have two polarities: ' Contracted resources look after their own skills development' to 'All our resources need to be at the highest level of competence. We have a part to play in ensuring that.'

There are many answers here, and many dependencies. Some factors to take into account are:

- the potential added value of the resource
- the need for team co-ordination and learning together
- the time commitment of the resource to the organisation
- involvement in the core competence of the organisation
- the individual's opportunity for self-development.

The nature of the help given may include:

- invitations to team learning events
- technical updates
- 'bonuses' in the form of learning credits to be used on company courses
- free books and media information/data
- access to learning resource centres.

> What kinds of non-core resources do you employ in your organisation? List for each the approach to its development that is adopted, and the resource's alternative means of personal growth. How might greater benefit accrue to your organisation by changing the levels of provision?

One extreme case might be the software programmer who works on a team for two years. He or she is indistinguishable from other employees except in terms of contract, pay rate and benefits. As far as work and contribution are concerned, his or hers is as important as that of any other member of the team. So one would expect participation in everything the team learns and in all its training. If such a person has an appraisal, however, it will probably focus on performance standards and short-term training needs rather than longer-term development.

Another situation might be the consultant who comes in

to do occasional training courses in his or her areas of specific expertise. A regular resource, he or she might need to keep in touch with organisational developments, progress and strategies – and in addition be involved in the sharing of learning that takes place in the group.

By contrast, the temporary secretary who comes in for four weeks from an agency may find that she or he has to look after her or his own skill development – unless the agency itself provides ongoing training.

How helpful will we be to employees in further education?

We have to decide:

■ what kinds of further education we should support, either because it is relevant to our business or in accordance with a policy of encouraging continual learning and development for employees

■ whether we should distinguish in terms of assistance between the two categories

■ what we should offer in terms of time and money

■ what level of discretion we should give to local managers.

'Accreditation' refers to certificates of achievement following a defined course approved by an authoritative external body. Sometimes a necessary passport to a specialist career or to client acceptance, it is also one of the routes to employability. This arena – in the UK – covers:

■ *professional qualification* – eg accountancy, personnel, purchasing, or chartered engineering. As a means of attracting staff, help may be promised towards the appropriate qualification – although the value placed on these attainments is variable. Because most of the people seeking help are young, most organisations help employees with both time and money. (It is common to pay 50 per cent of fees up front and 50 per cent on successful completion.) Membership fees will normally be paid for students, but not necessarily after qualification.

■ *Business qualification* – this used to embrace such certificates as the DMS (Diploma of Management Studies) and others, but today is strongly focused on the MBA (Master of Business Administration). MBAs come in many shapes and sizes, from the concentrated, in-depth, two-year, full-time course to the part-time, correspondence or virtual (via the Internet) degree. Most organisations (with exceptions among the major consulting firms) do not sponsor full-time MBAs because they know that the salary expectations will rise by 30 to 50 per cent (for a prestigious school), and they cannot cope with this internally. They will, however, fund part-time courses – totally or partially – often stipulating again that one half of the reimbursement is dependent on successful completion.

■ *National Vocational Qualifications (NVQs)* – this is another area where a policy will be needed. The choices concern which areas should be supported by the organisation and to what level, and how much they should be customised. Scottish and Newcastle Breweries, for example, invested an immense amount of effort in 1996–7 to customise NVQs for pub management, and found a direct relationship between pub success, employee motivation and the level of qualifications obtained by the staff. However, many organisations are put off by the bureaucracy and complexity that can be involved. For an excellent summary of NVQs see Rosemary Harrison's book, *Employee Development* (London, IPD, 1997, pp80–85).

To what extent shall we fund general personal development?

If we have a policy to support staff and encourage them in managing their own development and careers, we must make choices in the level of support that can be provided. Some of the questions to be answered include:

■ Should we invest in learning resource centres? If so, how many? How broad-ranging would the materials be? When should we provide access?

■ Should we provide career development workshops or counselling? To what extent would they be voluntary? Would people be left to themselves afterwards or should we provide mentoring or further support?

■ Should we fund non-business-related personal development? Should this be done by allocating a sum of money to each individual (as for example at Bodyshop and Rover), or should we provide a 'pot' for allocation/negotiation by managers? Should we place any boundaries on what will be funded?

One way to encourage personal development is to offer 'prizes' or 'bonuses' for job-related achievements which are learning-related. Thus a 'sum of money to be spent on books or a course' may be offered, or a visit to another part of the organisation, or some opportunity linked with customers or suppliers.

Brainstorm with some colleagues how you might introduce new ways of encouraging personal development through prizes and incentives. How would they be introduced and would there be any barriers to be overcome?

Do we want a specific policy on mentoring?

The policy on mentoring in the organisation may vary from none at all to the open provision of trained mentors to anyone who would like one. In the turbulence of organisations today an anchoring-point represented by an experienced person who is prepared to counsel and care seems very desirable. Many organisations are nowadays employing firms of experienced coaches to provide *external* mentoring, especially to senior people. There are a number of benefits in this, although it does point up some (inevitable?) gaps in the internal processes of dialogue in an organisation.

Questions for HRD to answer are:

- To whom should we offer this benefit?
- How consistent will this be with our stated beliefs on people development?
- To what extent should we train mentors and mentees?
- How should we manage the 'matching' process?
- What ongoing support should we provide for mentors?
- Should we encourage external mentors in some cases? And if so, how would this be managed?

> To whom does your organisation offer mentoring at the present time? What is the rationale behind choosing them and not others? How does your organisation's policy here reflect your general beliefs on people development?

How should we manage the recruitment and development of young people?

Guiding Principle 15

The variation in young entrants today no longer justifies organisations' talking about 'graduates' as if they were a homogeneous group.

Tertiary education is now available to so many more people that the range of 'qualified young entrants' is very broad. The range of positions for which they can be employed is broad too. Some are hired just to do a job. Others are hired specifically to provide the future leadership of the company. Job titles of those responsible for young-entrant recruitment and development (it is recommended that they are combined) are beginning to reflect this diversity. Questions for HRD are:

- What range of qualified people do we need, and for what?

- What approaches should we use for recruitment and selection?
- Should we manage all or part of the recruitment task centrally?
- What induction, training and development should we offer?
- How should we help with further professional qualifications?
- To what extent should we create special relationships with certain institutions, and what would the nature of that relationship be?

Surveys of graduates repeatedly show that training schemes feature strongly in their choices of organisation. The high loss rate many organisations experience is often due to unfulfilled expectations.

Table 17 on page 130 shows a matrix that can be built up. It is sometimes surprising when firms insist that every person must go through the same procedures, however obviously suitable they are, and allow their remuneration systems to eliminate the best people. If it is people that make the difference, surely there can be no other strategy in recruitment but to *try* to get the best possible candidates.

> How do you rate your success in the market in attracting and retaining good-quality young entrants? Draw up this matrix for your organisation. Do you feel you differentiate sufficiently in the various columns? What might you change?

When people move up (or across) the organisation, do we want any 'rites of passage'?

Prescribed series of 'events' that people attend at certain points in their careers are still widespread in large organisations. These may be triggered by a new level of management responsibility, or be modules of core competence training. Over time, managers and staff may

Table 17

A POLICY MATRIX FOR YOUNG-ENTRANT RECRUITMENT AND DEVELOPMENT

Type of young entrant	Target positions	Recruit-ment methods	Selection methods	Remuner-ation policy	Training schemes
MBA					
PhD					
Specialist Masters					
High-quality first degree					
Typical degree					
Lower tertiary qualification					
School-leaving qualifications					

be expected to collect a 'portfolio' of personal skills.

Many courses become enshrined in the culture and bestow their own status. There is always a need to update the relevance of these courses, and in fact a great amount of HRD spend may be devoted to them. However, as the emphasis grows on learning and self-management, the content of the courses may be less important than the benefits of creating networks of people who can benefit from each other's experience across the organisation.

For certain groups, these events may be external. Some well-known companies routinely send executives at a certain point in their careers for the three-month course at Harvard, or to a senior executive programme elsewhere. Others partner with a school to provide, for example, an executive MBA or regular customised courses that people are expected to attend. The choice is over the mix of external thinking that is sought, either for individuals or for managerial groups. An open course broadens the individual mind most of all but may provide the least ability to generate change. On the other hand, creating a common language and approach for managers as a group may be a powerful change catalyst.

> List all the established 'rites of passage' in your organisation. For each, how long has it been in existence? What measures are used to assess their benefit currently to the organisation? Are they the right measures and what do they tell us? Does this analysis provide any indicators for change?

Do we want any 'high-flyer programmes' and, if so, how should we position them?

Some organisations are very reluctant to indicate either to individuals or to the organisation at large that certain people are on 'accelerated development' or a designated 'high potential' scheme. This may be due to their reluctance to face the issues of labelling – that some have it and others do not – or to face the fact that people may not realise their potential as it had been perceived earlier. We have argued previously for a policy of openness. However, overt 'labelling' is best avoided as much as is feasible. One large international company describes its development programme for the few as 'career broadening'. Another calls its high-potential assessment centres 'career guidance', and every attender receives the same feedback and guidance regardless of whether his or her career path was seen as towards general management.

A related policy decision, if schemes exist, is 'nomination' v 'application'. The choice relates to the general beliefs and values of the organisation: if these reflect openness and personal ownership, then application must be allowed. This can be balanced by controlled *acceptance* – through entry standards and careful counselling.

In career development, how do we want to balance specialist v generalist development?

In many national and corporate cultures, development is highly specific right up to high levels. This creates a problem in the lack of overview that senior people have. Others decide (in different ways) that people should broaden at certain career stages. Yet others have no specific policy, and just let careers develop. Some of the different models employed may be summarised as follows:

■ *the narrow 'T'* – In this model people remain specialists until the highest level, managing groups of their own specialism but not working outside it. It is not until the top of the tree' that they take broader collegiate responsibilities (a system typical of Germany).

■ *the wide 'T'* – This is a commoner model in the UK, where beyond, say, the first 10 years of specialism and junior management people broaden across functional boundaries and become a 'management resource' thereafter.

■ *the 'T'* – Here young entrants are given a general knowledge of the organisation and its business for perhaps up to three years. They then specialise in a chosen area in which they remain until reaching senior management, when they become more general again.

■ *the double 'T'* – Starting as specialists, people are broadened through a variety of jobs and then settle into a specialism before finally broadening.

▌ *the 'Y' model* – Found in highly technical organisations, career opportunities and matching rewards exist to a more or less equally high level for both specialists and generalists.

> Which models are deployed deliberately, or implicitly, in your organisation? Do they meet the needs of the organisation's plans to develop strategically? If change would be helpful, what would be required to achieve it?

This is an important policy decision that has to be matched with rewards and that clearly influences people's ability to manage their own careers. One symptom of a problem is where good specialists become poor generalists because there is no alternative route for progress. If the organisation believes in the value of some varied experience, then it has to facilitate the movement across boundaries that is needed – some of which is not easy to 'self-manage'. SmithKline Beecham, for example, believes in the '2 functions plus 2 countries plus 2 business units' template for future general managers. Achieving this requires some planned career management.

The question to be answered, as always, is 'What mix of general/specialist experience will best serve the strategy of the organisation?' Most organisations today need expertise in their core competencies that is at least as critical a contributor as management capability.

How would 'equal opportunity' apply in HRD?

Every organisation today has some statement of equal opportunity. It may be a bland non-discriminating statement or more specific even positively discriminating. Public-sector organisations like to aim for an organisational distribution of race, gender, etc, that reflects the community in which they work. While this is laudable in principle, to force it through in practice runs the risk of many undesired inequities.

The more subtle issues here are not those of appointments and statistics. The danger of all statistics and averages is in the assumption that people have equal values and motivations about progression. True equal opportunity may mean valuing individual diversity and being flexible in the way we meet individual needs and life-balance requirements. Equal opportunity for *learning* would be a concern for the HRDM – including practical policies regarding continuous learning for those unable to have full-time contracts or on maternity leave.

The policy stating which levels of jobs should be openly advertised needs to be clarified (and enforced), and backed up with a procedure that is fair to all.

How do we want to balance internal promotion v external hire?

In order to perform effective manpower planning, the planned ratio of internal promotion to external hire is critical. It will be different depending on levels, and possibly on job groups also. Many of the 'built to last' companies mentioned earlier never recruit unless in exceptional circumstances beyond graduate level. They take more than they need at that point in order to allow for controlled attrition.

Others have a deliberate policy to bring in new blood constantly, and every vacancy is competed for on equal terms by internal and external candidates. Many state a deliberate desire to give first choice to their own people but make it clear that they will go outside when necessary.

Many managers seem convinced that the world outside is full of better people than they have, even though their own people leave and do much better outside – to their surprise. When we see that happening, there may be a lesson to be learned about our own development processes.

Few have a planned ratio that is built around their strategic needs and to which they seek to work. However, there is merit in it, especially in providing a target and standard for development activities.

> In the various parts of your organisation, what have been the historical ratios between internal and external resourcing at different levels? How many of these have been the result of a deliberate policy? How do they relate to loss rates and reasons for leaving? Can you draw any conclusions about whether a more planned approach would be of benefit?

In brief

■ Part of our strategy will be to formulate a set of policies that express our main beliefs in people development. Policies exist to provide more or less permanent sources of guidance to managers and employees.

■ The range and detail that is covered will reflect the level of direction or empowerment that organisations wish to give. Compared to general HR, there are a limited number of policy areas in HRD. However, they will be less administrative and more strategic.

■ So we have to decide how much variation and under what circumstances we shall allow variation. *Principles* should be common everywhere. But the application of them may vary with national situations, with different groups of employees and with historical situations arising from mergers. Our willingness to tolerate diversity will be a reflection of our general culture.

■ We looked at some of the considerations for decisions in a number of HRD policy areas.

■ Policy guidance is more necessary in development than training – because the former needs more consistency and synergy across different parts of the organisation. A policy on internal-promotion:external-hire ratios is of considerable help to an HRDM in development planning.

6
Prioritising and Resourcing

Prioritising the demands for learning

As we collect together all the learning needs from the drivers described in Chapter 3, we could be justified in arguing that *all* should be met because they are all business-driven. 'If you think training is expensive, try ignorance' is a saying attributed to the CEO of Motorola. Nevertheless, some activities are more critical than others, and some have a clearer and stronger return on investment. In reality, too, most HRDMs will have a budget and limited resources. Prioritising must be done and options for resourcing examined. What governs priorities?

It would be easy to say that short-term benefits to the organisation's bottom line come first. In a sense they do, but if we did a really thorough analysis of all the potential demands for increasing capability, we would absorb all our energy in that arena. So we need a balance. Development is more about ongoing consistent investment in processes (the only major cost being in the dedicated and intelligent time and effort of a small number of professionals, plus that contributed by line managers), whereas training is more diverse. Of course, like other good things in life, much learning comes 'free' – if only we can harness it.

Accountants work in yearly cycles (mostly). Life is not like that, however. If we are to respond to business needs, we need to balance the planned learning needs with those that emerge during the year (such as a merger, a new piece of legislation, or a major competitive threat). We need systems and guidelines for making choices – both at the end of formal needs analysis and in weighing up new priorities. It is too easy, in the eagerness to be wanted and to please others, to say yes to every request that comes in or that results from legitimate consultancy activity. The same syndrome affects salespeople, where the joy of a sale may well exceed its actual value to the organisation in profit contribution!

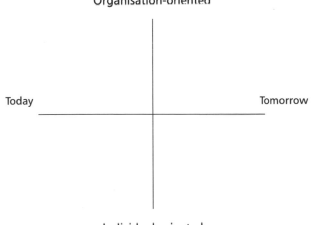

Guiding principle 16

Always plan and budget in a way that allows for response to emerging needs through the year.

Figure 6 shows a matrix that needs to be balanced in choosing our eventual portfolio.

Figure 6

BALANCED PRIORITIES IN PEOPLE DEVELOPMENT

Organisation-oriented

Today

Tomorrow

Individual-oriented

Ideally, we should have some activities in each quartile. However, the top left-hand may dominate a shareholder-value-focused company and may also be rejected by HRD as too focused on boring, unexciting business areas that we do not understand very well. We therefore need some methods of deciding priorities that will stand up to scrutiny by any inquirer in the organisation.

Cost-benefit analysis

Costs are relatively easy to understand, calculate and forecast. The allocation of overheads is always tricky, and we may need to deploy some activity-based costing. Benefits and returns, whether financial or otherwise, are more difficult – for two reasons: firstly, they are often difficult to attribute solely to the learning activity undertaken, and secondly, they are often 'indirect' rather than visibly appearing in the performance measures of the organisation.

Table 18 shows the kind of format that could be used to sort out priorities, at least as an input to the final judgement that has to be made. This may be difficult to complete for the longer-term, developmental, softer-skills interventions but is more designed to allow choices in the demands for training. It starts with an immediate question regarding performance indicators to be affected (ie improved), and this focuses the mind. The 'non £' columns may require some narrative, but still need to be strongly business-related.

Approximations are better than nothing, so long as they have credibility. Often estimates of percentage increases or decreases are easier to come by than absolute figures. For teambuilding, leadership and other softer skills, if the training has had a positive effect we would expect to see an increase in *productivity* of the team or the group that is being led – and this can be targeted and measured.

Table 18

SETTING PRIORITIES FOR THE TRAINING PORTFOLIO

Programme/ intervention	Performance indicators to be affected	Year one benefit (£)	Year one benefits (non £)	Year two benefit (£)	Year two benefits (non £)	Cost £	Cost-benefit balance	Long-term impact (H/M/L)	Priority H/M/L

H/M/L = High/Medium/Low

Priority-setting is not an exact science – it is also pragmatic and political. We do not like to say no to requests – even if they are clearly not a good use of our resources – especially if we see a longer-term relationship at stake or an entry-point into a previously difficult area. But a systematic starting-point is the mark of the professional.

> What criteria do you use for deciding priorities? To what extent do you evaluate cost and benefits systematically? Could you develop a better system than you have?

When it comes to *development* the same principles will apply. Here we are talking more about processes that will have some considerable life. Priorities will be determined by the resource needed to set up, and then maintain, the processes, and by the target population. Thus in a part of the population such as graduates, if we neglect attention to development we shall find we soon lose most of our recruits and therefore our initial investment.

Choices in resourcing

Many a strategy fails in its implementation because the resources needed were not fully understood or available. Financial funds are always finite and competed for. However, they are not the only resource about which decisions need to be made – indeed the funds sought will be dependent on some of the choices in other areas. We look at the following:

- where to carry out HRD activities
- equipping the activities
- organisation, people and their capability
- networks
- funding strategies.

Where should we carry out our activities?

Many well-known organisations maintain large, centralised training establishments, some with grand names. These serve many purposes in addition to their main function, which is to provide an environment for training to take place. They bring people together from different parts of the organisation and are used for different types of meetings, corporate celebrations or rituals. Some see them as a luxury or as inconsistent with the core businesses of the organisation, and many have either been sold as cost-cutting exercises or become revenue-earning centres for use by other organisations.

It is likely that the decision to acquire, maintain or sell such a centre will not be in the hands of the HRDMs. However, they will certainly have a strong interest in it, and it will significantly affect the job they do. What factors govern such a decision?

The need to have the most cost-effective delivery of training

Cost calculations can be done to compare different ways of delivering training. Readers are referred to books by Fitz-Enz (see Further Reading), founder of the Saratoga Institute, for detailed approaches to costing HRD programmes.

We should beware of the trap of believing that because costs are adequately recovered *internally* the facility is therefore cost-effective. Calculations must take a company-wide view. The considerations to be taken into account include whether the organisation's own premises or some external facilities are to be used.

Own premises

∎ premises costs – rent or ownership costs, utilities, services

∎ equipment purchase and depreciation

∎ catering costs

■ travel for company delegates

■ extent of subsidy obtainable through external revenues by allowing others to use the facility

■ facilities management cost and time.

External facilities

■ delegate day-rates, including all-in room hire and meals

■ special equipment hire

■ travel for company delegates

■ travel and accommodation for training staff.

One cannot predict any general outcome of such calculations because every organisation's situation will be different. Where a large amount of standard training has to be delivered it is likely that the economics will swing in favour of having a dedicated site. For monitoring purposes, ratios such as 'cost per training day delivered' will provide a suitable measure.

It is worth emphasising here that the standard training course is *not* necessarily an effective way of learning. Particularly when there is a goal to maximise utilisation of facilities and trainers, there is a natural tendency to 'fit' courses into standard lengths. So many courses take 4.5 days, and this may have nothing to do with what is necessary for the learning to take place. One of the advantages of not having an owned facility is that this tendency is much reduced, and because external costs are so much more visible, there is pressure in the *opposite* direction. The training facility also has a vested interest in encouraging courses *per se*, rather than other forms of learning. The HRDM needs to have overall control of this resource in order to keep the right balance. A good costs comparison will therefore bring in factors that reflect these tendencies, and the only way to do this is to 'zero-base' all the training that is done.

> Pick a variety of events that are being currently run as off-the-job programmes. What are their learning objectives? What alternative ways of achieving those objectives might be available? Form a view of the cost/effectiveness balance of the alternatives.

The benefit of getting people in the organisation to learn from each other

Learning is not just in classrooms but is live and dynamic between people. A common centre is an enabler of learning about other parts of the organisation, of the sharing of good practice and the making of contacts that will be useful in the future. This is perhaps the most significant benefit of all – and cannot be quantified.

The benefit from having training staff co-located with their place of delivery

This is a mixed blessing. Clearly, there are benefits from the closeness to facilities, for the ability to utilise training staff productively and for being able to create a team and departmental spirit. But these establishments tend to be quite pleasant and relaxed, and provide a very comfortable working environment. This is not a problem in itself, of course, but can lead to complacency among staff and a strong vested interest in its continuation.

The benefit of a corporate cultural centre as a means of cohesion

Many a manager and many an employee have a special fondness for their training centre. Full of memories, both social and to do with learning, they may look forward to every visit. The centre may be an environment that provides some escape from the everyday grind, where people from different parts of the company can be met and talked to, and where somehow the spirit of the company can be found. The 'real' culture and values live in the bars and dining rooms and leisure facilities of the organisation's training centre. Even the presence of 'paying guests' – external revenue-providers – seems not to diminish the sense of ownership that people feel. Accountants do not generally take account of such 'soft' benefits when doing their evaluations. The question of balance is the extent to which this feeling of cohesion is *positive* in promoting the desired culture, or whether it perpetuates an old way of being that is inappropriate for the future.

By contrast to the 'bricks and mortar' visible to everybody, a *virtual* centre of learning may enjoy some of the benefits of centralisation, at least economically. It loses out on the 'club' aspect, on learning from and with colleagues, but is better able to be customised and is 'just-in-time'. It is best not seen as an alternative but more as a potential addition to the learning resources available.

What should we do about equipment?

Having a training centre of one's own can mean a large expenditure on equipment. If highly specialised equipment is fundamental, such as cockpit simulators or mainframe computers, then this is about core competence and must be done. For more general training, the days of a few flipcharts and OHPs have now been replaced with computer presentation projectors, wireless simultaneous-response receivers, multimedia PCs as learning machines, and so on. The utilisation of much of the equipment purchased may be low but is rarely monitored. Often hire on a 'just-in-time' basis may be more efficient.

Learning resource centres (sometimes called 'Open learning centres')

The main establishment is not the only candidate for capital. In order to support a strategic approach to personal learning, there may be a project to establish and equip 'learning resource centres' at one or more sites that enable employees to learn at their own pace and maybe to take a course of their own choosing. A learning resource centre will normally have a range of equipment – PCs, interactive video, audio – together with libraries of videos, tapes, books and workbook materials. The South West Electricity Board estimated the cost of setting up one centre to be £80,000 – and then found it very rarely used: an experience shared by many. Studies made by the Learning Sharefair (a network of companies sharing experiences in the learning arena) found that:

- It was not difficult to sell the concept and the 'investment' to senior management.
- However, people needed the motivation to utilise the centre, and rarely did so merely 'out of interest'.
- Busy people, especially managers, preferred to learn in spare time away from work.

So HRD should be cautious before following a popular fashion, and take some lessons from the marketing department before major investments.

Organisation, people and their capability

People are without doubt our most important resource in HRD. We need a range of roles and skills for HRD to be effective through the organisation, and they will not all be under the control of the HRDM. So the way people development is co-ordinated, recognising all the different contributors, is just as critical as the skills available in HRD itself.

HRD must work with the organisation that exists (which may be often changing). It needs a very clear 'map' of accountabilities and how they interact between the contributors. In a central position, close liaison with devolved units responsible for HRD matters is essential, and a clear understanding of roles and expectations by all parties. In a subsidiary position, the reverse will apply. Far too much time is wasted in organisations through boundary 'disputes' – time that should be used creatively and positively.

The *role* of the HRDM is to understand the drivers of learning in the organisation, to translate them to learning needs, to direct the professional meeting of them, and to ensure that HRD continually adds value to the organisation. The *job title* used will be affected by the value system and philosophy on people development. Some options are (for *manager* we might read *director*):

■ *Manager, human resource development* – This goes well with an HR approach to people, and is a suitably all-embracing term. Some organisations would want the title to reflect their particular philosophy, however.

■ *Training and development manager* – This again is general, but the emphasis on training might not reflect the culture desired.

■ *Learning and development manager* – This is a variation that is common today – with a deliberate emphasis on learning.

■ *Management development manager* – In some organisations this is the only HRD role title found at a central level. However, it may give the message that managers are more important than other employees.

■ *Managing or senior partner, learning consultancy* – This may be appropriate in a totally consultancy-focused function. However, the use of 'partner' has legal implications and should be deployed with caution.

■ *Human assets manager, intellectual capital development manager, etc* – Increasingly the recognition of the intellectual capital in people is being reflected in job titles.

Titles have political implications and affect the impression that people have of what someone contributes. Accuracy in reflecting what is done may not be the first consideration!

HRD organisation

For many readers this may be a given, because HRD comprises only one person or is very small. Individuals have to embrace a wide variety of activities and have to be skilled at deciding which merit their personal attention, which can be outsourced and which cannot be resourced at all.

In larger organisations some of the questions that arise are:

- How do we see the total HRD resource across the organisation?
- To what extent should training and development activities be integrated?
- How should HRD interface with the organisation?
- Do we want to run primarily as a supplier or as a consultancy?

How do we see the total HRD resource across the organisation?

This will reflect organisational structure, culture and values, although HRD is in a unique position to break down rigidity and boundaries if thought desirable. We may have a central resource dedicated to cross-company programmes and not involved with the day-to-day training and development needs of people and teams. Its prime focus would be on organisational learning, on policy and global processes. Out in the units are the people who run the activities that are needed locally. Every now and then they all meet together and discuss areas of common interest.

This division between central and local has the benefit of dedicated accountability, but can lead to isolation of any part, and duplication between units. An alternative is to see all HRD as an integrated resource, and to share ownership of central programmes' field-based staff. At the very least it is recommended that the specialist expertise that each practitioner has is publicised for the benefit of all. In my time at ICL, we took some hundred specialist subjects, grouped under Learning, Organisation Development, Career Management, Performance Management, Skills and Qualifications, Resourcing, and 'General'. Each subject had a 'focus person' who took the lead in professional expertise (they might have been in HR or HRD anywhere in the world), and then up to five others could designate themselves as 'specially interested'. This 'Register of Expertise' was electronically available to all.

To what extent should training and development activities be integrated?

In some organisations these are quite separate. Training has its own director, staff and facilities, and the development side of HRD may be handled by a small number of specialists or by HR managers themselves. Others see people development as an integrated function and discuss training and development issues at the same time with units. A consultancy-focused organisation would certainly do this, and should have all HRD activities integrated.

How should HRD interface with the organisation?

There are three basic options:

- *by subgroups that have common development needs* across the organisation as a whole. Thus HRD would have staff dedicated to salespeople, management, clerical staff, etc, and their overall needs. If this is chosen, the integrated approach to training and development makes sense.

- *by organisational unit* – for all the staff in one unit. This has the advantage of strong client relationships, and the HRD 'relationship manager' can develop a strong affinity for the activities, problems and people of a unit.

- *by subject area* – organised by skill or expertise, each person or group offers a range of consultancy or events available to all. This would be the structure of the traditional training department, allied to the first option but focused on training.

In practice, a combination of these may be chosen. Thus a person responsible for a subject area may also take the role of relationship manager for one or more units.

Do we want to run primarily as a supplier or as a consultancy?

We cannot avoid doing some of both. Indeed, it is dangerous to see this as black and white, and – for example – to suddenly abandon the course catalogue in an effort to show people a new consultancy mode. 'Customers' may not think as radically as HRD and may have expectations that need time to adjust. Also, inevitably, there will be some regularly run scheduled events dealing with core capabilities and continuing skill enhancement needs. But the *primary* choice will radically affect the skills on which we focus, the eventual portfolio of activities, the measures of success, and the whole HRD culture.

> Consider the HRD organisational structure of which you are part. What do you see as its advantages and disadvantages? What 'non-added-value' activities does it need to keep it functioning? Would any alternative models be beneficial?

Roles in the HRD community

There is scope for a number of roles, and no individual should expect to be skilled in them all. The range needed will clearly depend on the *structural* choices made.

Guiding principle 17

In people development we need to remember that it is not only HRD-dedicated staff that are contributing. The task is to clarify the roles of all involved and equip them with the skills they need to manage their part.

Professional trainers are those who – either by virtue of their subject expertise, or because of their interest in the training process – have made training their career. A range of specific competencies apply to them, including:

- training design
- materials design
- classroom delivery
- group facilitation
- individual coaching
- evaluation.

Trainers may be *internal* or *external*, and we look at the merits of these options below.

Learning consultants are experts in the process of learning, and in the choice of learning needs and solutions. Their consultancy skills are central to them – coupled with a strong background knowledge of the organisation and its goals, of the nature of the workplace and its pressures and demands, and of how people learn. They should be skilled in translating a problem (or opportunity) into learning needs, at any level in the organisation. This is more than just being an expert in learning itself: it involves understanding the language, the pressures and the demands of the business. Many trainers tend to believe the task takes care of itself, and problems need to be seen essentially in *people* terms. The effective consultant is knowledgeable enough to assess task, system *and* people components of a problem.

Managing consultants – In a consultancy-led HRD function there is scope for a senior role to co-ordinate other consultants in a specialist area. Consultants may move around specialist teams, depending on their own development plans. This role might also take on that of 'relationship manager' (or 'client manager') as needs and structure dictate.

Programme and project managers – HRD always has some ongoing programmes for which it is responsible. Examples include:

- graduate development
- high-potential assessment
- high-potential development
- general management development
- continuity-planning
- organisational change initiatives
- special skill change initiatives.

The HRDM may take personal responsibility for some of these, or delegate them to others. External people may assist with delivery, but ownership will always want to be with the HRD function itself.

Guiding Principle 18

Developing people takes time. Continuity in directing programmes is fundamental to success and, particularly in management development, an incumbency of at least three years is recommended.

Managing development programmes is not a 'paper' job – the person responsible needs to get out and meet as many as possible of the people he or she is seeking to develop and to understand their individual situations and contexts.

Project managers are needed also for change management programmes or other special initiatives, such as looking at the intellectual capital of a merger, joint venture or acquisition. Unlike the above, who may take accountability for several programmes, project managers should be single-minded and dedicated, so that they wake up in the morning and worry about only one set of tasks.

Support staff – Essential contributors, these include event administrators, materials controllers, marketing staff and secretaries. The ratio of this group to the other categories is an important measure of efficiency, but if too low it can be seriously counter-productive. Creative people who can design learning materials and make them exciting and interesting in different media are also valuable, although it may be that they cannot be resourced in-house.

HR managers – If the HRDM sits centrally in an organisation, operational HR managers (where they exist) may sometimes be seen as a barrier on account of their gate-keeping role. We look at the politics of this in Chapter 7, but ideally HR managers should be seen as partners and a resource in their own right. Their role can include acting as:

■ agents of the HRD strategy
■ champions of the desired learning culture
■ a source of learning needs
■ effective implementers of the HRD systems and processes
■ deliverers of certain learning solutions.

Line managers – It is often the case that the HRD specialists live in another world from that of line managers. After all, they think about learning issues all day, whereas for managers such issues may be low in their time allocation. (Despite exhortations to be more concerned about developing their people, the pressures put on most managers will ensure that this situation does not change much.) However, they do have a unique and vital part in the learning and development of the people who work with and for them because they decide who does what in the daily work.

For all managers, to be skilled in understanding how learning can support their business goals would be a very helpful capability. (This does not feature too often in the managerial skills portfolio, which is more likely to include coaching and feedback.)

The strategy of your organisation may be that every person should take ownership of his or her own learning and development. If so, you will know that it takes a long time, especially in complex organisations, for this to be a firmly embedded reality. It is more likely to be found in departments where a particular line and/or HR manager has made it a priority, or in smaller enterprises. Even if it is achieved, the manager or team leader is in no way isolated from the learning process of the people who work with him or her. But the manager becomes a supporter rather than a controller in the process. A prime goal is to ensure that all staff are trained in how to manage learning for themselves, and that they have a live and dynamic personal development plan.

The manager's role in a 'learning environment' is described well by Honey and Mumford in their 1996 manual *Managing in a Learning Environment*, looking at four parameters:

▪ being a role model of learning himself or herself
▪ being a conscious and generous provider of learning opportunities for others
▪ building learning into the daily systems of work
▪ being a champion for learning across the organisation.

The questionnaire which they use to assess these factors is helpful and enlightening – although I have often found when using it that managers respond by saying 'It is all very well and desirable, but where do we get the time to be so perfect?' This is a very real problem, and it is a task of the HRDM to be realistic and build into his or her expectations and processes that which can be practically achieved by the majority of managers.

Line managers are resources in other ways. They may be mentors to others (particularly younger people such as graduates), assessors in development centres, resources in training exercises, and givers of their own experience in learning events. Unless the organisation has a detailed time-based cross-charging system, they are a 'free' resource to HRD.

> Draw up a summary of the respective roles of HRD staff, HR, the line manager and the individual in the people development arena today. Is there a case for any adjustment of these roles, and what would be the implications for capability for each of the contributors?

The HRDM would want to be sure that any competency profiles for line manager positions – or indeed *any* position – recognised the need to support the strategy of the organisation through people development.

Mentors – A network of mentors throughout the organisation can fulfil a critical role where emphasis is put on personal ownership of development. In some organisations mentoring is made available to all. HRD would be responsible for managing the network and mentor capability. Readers are recommended to study the specialist books on this area published by the IPD (see Further Reading).

What are the capabilities needed by professional HRD staff?

We have emphasised the importance of capability frameworks for managing development effectively, and HRD should be a role model in their use.

The HRDM

The HRDM must have a very special profile. Not only should he or she be expert in understanding learning and in managing learning processes but he or she must also talk the language of the organisation's business fluently. That means an appreciation of the underlying 'technology' of the organisation, the issues incurred in managing it, and the key roles and activities that are necessary. Above all, familiarity with the numbers that drive the organisation is essential, and the ability to make cost and benefit calculations with credibility. Add to this the attributes of sociability, influencing, consultancy, listening, organisational sensitivity, risk-taking and functional leadership – and adding a heavy dose of passionate pleasure in seeing people develop – and we have a scarce combination!

It will have been a considerable advantage to have worked 'in the line', but my observation is that seconding line managers who do *not* have a passion for people development or a real understanding of how people learn is a disaster. If they cannot lead the function professionally, they will rapidly lose the respect of the staff.

HRD staff

One organisation that has recognised the need for a range of roles in HRD uses a 'T' framework for describing the total capability set needed, as shown in Figure 7 on page 156. Each capability has descriptions of five levels of expertise.

> Do you have an HRD capability framework? If not, what would be its basic structure? If so, how well does it meet the needs of the values, structure and roles that HRD needs? Study some 'person specifications' for HRD staff in other organisations and see if there are some ideas to apply to yourself.

One individual does not need to have all of these capabilities, and indeed is unlikely to do so. It is a common mistake to expect developers to be competent over such a wide range.

Each role will have some *core* skills that are the foundation of the capability needed, and would build into the overall HRD capability framework. Table 19 on page 157 shows some examples for consultant roles.

Figure 7

A CAPABILITY PROFILE FOR HRD STAFF

Consultancy skills	Personal skills	Project management
Facilitation skills	Teamwork	Bid management
Change management	Business/commercial awareness	Programme management
	Learning needs analysis	
	Diagnostics	
	Developing and delivering learning solutions	
	Subject expertise	

Table 19

EXAMPLE OF CORE CAPABILITIES FOR CONSULTANTS

All consultants	Managing consultants
∎ a desire and ability to help others	∎ credibility with sponsors and clients
∎ subject matter expertise related to a product set	∎ business management skills
∎ supplementary supportive expertise	∎ people development skills
∎ ability as a consultant	∎ programme management skills
∎ integrity	∎ portfolio vision and direction
∎ self-managing expertise	∎ a passion for building a learning culture
∎ adding value continuously to the practice	∎ judgement as to when to say 'No, sorry'

Staffing calculations

In staffing, the HRDM needs to plan for the number of person days for each capability at each level – for example:

∎ n person days of capability X at Level A

∎ m person days of capability Y at Level B

∎ p person days of capability Z at Level B.

An example of building up a resource requirement is shown in Table 20 on page 158. Note these are *person days*. Each *individual* may use several capabilities in a time period.

Table 20

IN-HOUSE RESOURCE PLAN

Period: January–June 2000	Available:	10 persons × 182 days × 70 per cent utilisation = 1,274 days
Capability	*Level*	*Person days needed*
Learning consultancy	Expert	127
Learning consultancy	Distinguished	80
Project management	Competent	56
Developing and delivering solutions	Distinguished	318
Developing and delivering solutions	Competent	318
Bid management	Distinguished	60
Facilitation	Distinguished	60
Facilitation	Competent	125
Programme management	Distinguished	100
Diagnostics	Expert	30

Note this uses the simple competency level classification referred to earlier:

A = Aware; B = Basic; C = Competent; D = Distinguished; E = Expert

> If you do not do resource planning on this kind of basis, have a look at what your current portfolio requires. Try to draw from this some methodology that would help you in more competent capability planning, especially utilising the different levels of expertise.

HRD people need continual development themselves. Time and money must be allowed for individual development, team development and internal sharing. Typical figures might be four team days per year and a further eight to ten days per person – but the latter should vary with individual need and be negotiated as part of a personal development plan.

Networks

Networks are an important resource both to the HRDM himself or herself and within the organisation. If the HRDM sees an accountability for knowledge transfer across the organisation, and recognises the need to 'create bridges across boundaries', he or she should work with business areas and functions to facilitate people's coming together. The HRDM should make a map of what is happening across the organisation: where are there flows of both person-to-person and electronic communication? This check-list may be used:

Department/division:

- What are the boundaries that potentially prevent people sharing together?
- In what ways and how often do they come together face-to-face now?
- In what ways and how often do they communicate electronically?
- Who would be the catalysts for creating network activities?
- How can HRD help to facilitate them?

Perhaps a reader might respond by saying, 'But this is not *my* problem!' The question is 'How accountable does the HRDM feel for organisational learning?' If the ultimate accountability is to ensure it is maximised, the learning from others is a major contributor. So HRD may both initiate and manage networks itself – learning networks that follow up, as a group, a particular programme, or common interest groups (such as people interested in self-managed learning). The possibilities are endless and – like Internet newsgroups – the goal is that they have a life of their own and need only occasional stimulation.

How many networks is HRD involved in internally? What other opportunities can you see for initiating, facilitating or regenerating others?

The HRDM will want to learn from others, too, and others external to the organisation. Good external networks and clubs are a key resource – for benchmarking, for finding out about good practice, for questioning one's approach and getting new ideas, and for 'plagiarising' from others. 'Network' is included in our components of capability as distinctive and critical.

Some useful networks for HRD are shown in Table 21.

Table 21

USEFUL NETWORKS FOR HRD MANAGERS

Association of Management Educators and Developers (AMED) 0171 235 3505
(www.management.org.uk)

European Foundation of Management Development (efmd) 00322 6480385
(www.efmd.be)

American Society of Training and Development (ASTD) 001 783 683 8100
(www.astd.org)

Learning Sharefair 01628 623456
(100417.1127@compuserve.com)

European Human Resource Forum (ehrf) 01934 863331
(ehrf@cix.co.uk)

The Conference Board Europe 0032 2 675 5405
(www.conference-board.organisation)

Careers Research Forum 0171 470 7104
(email @crforum.co.uk)

Institute of Personnel and Development Forums 0181 263 3257
(www.ipd.co.uk)

> How many networks do you and your colleagues belong to, internally and externally?

Funding strategies

Money is, of course, the most critical resource needed. Money for most organisations has to be found internally, but it may also be sourced externally either from bodies with funds to dispense (such as the EU) or from external revenue-generating activities from internal resources.

External revenue generation

External revenues can come from:

■ letting out facilities and/or equipment – utilising spare capacity and maximising the return on fixed costs

■ selling places on internal training courses – this is commonly done on technical courses, where know-how is the main learning goal, or on routine skills courses. It is inappropriate for events where open discussion on the organisation is needed.

■ providing external client consultancy – utilising spare capacity of learning consultants or trainers on external client opportunities

■ licensing training methodologies or selling materials – where these are not deemed to be of competitive advantage

■ providing HRD services to other organisations – 'insourcing' – utilising fixed costs and resources to provide service to other organisations as well as the homebase.

Some of these activities are very attractive to managers and staff, as well as to senior management for the resource productivity they bring. They enable entrepreneurialism without risk. There are many potential advantages to those involved:

- sharpening consultancy skills in a commercial environment
- learning business skills first-hand
- keeping an external focus.

The danger is clear, however: people whose prime task is to meet the needs of the *organisation* get more fun from working externally. It develops them personally, gives them pride in generating revenue, and keeps them from the daily politics and trials of organisational life. Furthermore, when successful, management sets revenue targets, linked to bonuses, and this activity dominates priorities.

My own experience in this area has led me to the following Guiding Principle:

Guiding principle 19

If there is good potential for external revenue to be made from training activities, keep the resources involved as far as is feasible separate from those dedicated to internal learning.

Many companies have realised that they have created some internal excellence in some training areas and that this may be of interest to other organisations – first to existing customers but then going beyond that. Most of the IT companies have external training organisations, specialising in IT areas but branching out into others too. ICL named its training business 'Peritas' and gave it a very broad remit; British Airways spun out its 'Speedwing Training' after its success in its own quality service programme. Another example is the small Bedfordshire company, Dutton's Engineering, which, after some years of highly focused and successful training, created a division called Business Excellence Training 'committed to the provision of high-quality training which will enable organisations to achieve excellence by realising the potential of their people'.

Where both external and internal exist, staff can move between each 'side' (because the advantages outlined above are real and worth while) but should not be asked to serve two masters at one time – the needs of the organisation will lose out. However, because there are advantages in external exposure, one might allow, say, up to five to ten days' external work a year.

Internal funding

Internal funding is a very political matter, and the HRDM will be subject to organisational accounting rules. Options and their effects include those in Table 22:

Table 22

FUNDING MECHANISMS FOR HRD

Mode of funding	Advantages	Disadvantages
1 Centrally funded as an overhead cost; resources cut to that budget and events provided free to users	▪ stability, clarity, ease of planning ▪ reinforces importance of training and development ▪ not subject to 'client' unit budget difficulties	▪ no ownership by units, so use of events may not be taken seriously ▪ central focus may not meet the real needs ▪ risk of complacency by HRD
2 Funded through negotiated annual contributions from units	▪ relatively stable for planning purposes ▪ units have ownership of their budget ▪ opportunity to create internal client relationships	▪ assumes the nature of demand does not change through the year ▪ risk of renegotiation especially when reorganisation takes place

continued on page 164

Table 22 (*continued*)

FUNDING MECHANISMS FOR HRD

Mode of funding	Advantages	Disadvantages
3 Combination of (1) and (2) with a 'central subsidy' (for strategic programmes and/or making the use of internal resources attractive financially)	▌ combines the advantages of (1) and (2) ▌ judicious application of central subsidies enables priorities to be given to strategic change and cross-organisational issues	▌ has some of the disadvantages of (1) and (2), but to a lesser extent
4 Free market approach – departments contract event by event and pay the advertised price	▌ able to be really responsive to the needs of units ▌ no scope for HRD to 'peddle its own agenda'	▌ a lot of time is spent in selling and negotiating ▌ no ability to plan resources – so will keep in-house to a minimum ▌ 'numbers' overtake quality ▌ difficulty in giving any cohesive messages across the organisation ▌ becomes a supplier rather than a support for the strategies

There are variations of these basic positions. As you go from position 1 to 4 it becomes more and more difficult to be 'strategic', and HRD becomes progressively more involved in daily planning and number-balancing. On the other hand, if HRD is a central service, and if the organisation is very much devolved so that business units are very different and the level of cross-organisational synergy is very low, it can be a very appropriate model.

One critical factor in the funding equation is the freedom given to units to use external suppliers as against the internal option. In some organisations this freedom is zero:

if an internal option is there, it must be used. In others the freedom to make a choice between alternatives is total. The problem of the latter is that there is a strange psychological tendency for units to believe the grass is greener externally and to reject an internal option just because it is internal. Rationality may not rule!

Pricing

Sources of funds are one thing, but how those funds are allocated to activities is another. Pricing is a strategic tool itself. Some options are shown in Table 23:

Table 23

PRICING OPTIONS

Pricing approach	Objective	Comments
1 Standard training dayrate	Simplicity, volume, 'bums on seats'	Focus is on cost rather than value; training as a commodity
2 Activity-based cost price	To reflect true costs of development and delivery	This is better, but problem of forecasting product life for development recovery; also more work involved
3 Consultancy-based price, at cost	Straight, no-frills internal price	Value of offering may not be appreciated
4 Consultancy-based price, at market rate less discount(s)	To demonstrate both true value and benefit of internal customer	Gives flexibility to control messages
5 Consultancy-based price, at market rate	To demonstrate value of solution offered and awareness of market	Places HRD firmly in competitive market

The first question is whether HRD or the training department is expected to make an internal profit or to subsidise some activities from others. Internal profit-making is generally not recommended. It is an unnecessary source of conflict and game-playing, and adds no value to the organisation or its customers. Subsidising low-price or free activities from high-price ones may sometimes be helpful – for example, pump-priming a network, sponsoring some internal departmental development, or handling some unbudgeted but important need. However, although pragmatic, this is not ideal, and it is better to have specifically reserved funds in the budget for such needs.

There will always be a portfolio of 'standard' courses, and these can be priced on a standard basis. The key parameter in such pricing will be 'lecturer productivity'. The ratio of these to 'non-standard', 'once-off', pilot or bespoke events will vary between organisations. If HRD has decided to run itself as a consultancy, then it will have standard fee rates per person as a basis of costing. These fee rates will be a person's salary marked up for the actual overhead costs of running the HRD department – non-revenue earning days, management, premises, marketing and support staff. These should be allocated using an activity-based costing method, and may typically double the all-in salary cost.

Some events may be 'free' to all participants because they are centrally funded. (The most common approach here is that individual units pay for travel and accommodation only. This tends to disadvantage poorer units or units at a long distance, so they may need to be subsidised.) Typical centrally funded programmes are high-potential development centres and educational programmes, senior management development, change management programmes and graduate development.

Pricing strategies 3, 4 and 5 above in Table 23 show different ways of pricing for consultancy. Just to do it at cost should certainly give a cheaper option to the client unit than an external proposal. To price at market rate means being market-competitive and making a profit. You might take this route for proposals that are not firmly in

HRD's 'added value portfolio' – but if you do, there is a risk that this would cause the client relationship to suffer.

Strategy 4 has merit. Price by value – ie market rate. Then the client unit sees the true market cost. This can then be discounted: say, 20–25 per cent would bring it down to cost as a standard 'internal discount'. Various subsidies can be applied – up to 100 per cent – if it can be paid for out of 'strategic funding'.

> Examine your funding and pricing strategies against the alternatives given. Can you see any merit in alternative approaches? Who would benefit and how? Be sure that overall the organisation would gain, rather than just HRD!

External v internal resources

Most organisations today do not expect to draw all their human capability from fully contracted employees, and training is one area where this is generally the case. There is a very wide range of suppliers available, specialised in particular fields, and an HRD department could not utilise full-time all the skills needed. The question for the HRDM is 'How do I decide the skills I should have in-house (if any)?'

This is not so much a cost decision as one of *value*. Where do in-house staff have the capacity to add value over and above that which can be obtained externally? Some possibilities are:

▌ They can have an in-depth understanding of the organisation, its people, its business and its strategies.

▌ They can share in the common business goals and loyalties.

▌ They can build a network of contacts within and outside the organisation.

■ They enable the transfer of learning and best practice across the organisation.

■ They can create centres of excellence that can be a competitive advantage.

A set of criteria can be drawn up to determine whether activities should be resourced in-house on this basis of value added.

Guiding Principle 20

If any demands on HRD do not pass the criteria for added value contribution from internal staff, external resources should be used.

These criteria, when combined with the activities plan, can help determine the number and skills of the resources needed. Of course, we may make a compromise against our set of criteria, sometimes for political reasons, but at least we should know we are doing that.

> Do you have a clear description of where added value comes from in-house staff? How does your current portfolio stack up to it? Did you make compromises, and if so, why?

Using business schools

Business schools and management colleges offer a number of opportunities to assist with development, particularly of managers. They offer a variety of MBA and Masters courses, varying in cost, quality, timing and content. These may be used by individuals (see page 126 in Chapter 5), or an organisation may work with a school on a customised version designed for its employees. Standards of accreditation will demand a heavy academic input. The 'International Management Schools' approach (a network of schools bonded by a focus on action learning) is much more project-based, but their degrees have not been formally recognised by the awarding powers.

The driving force of most traditional schools is research and not teaching, or even less 'learning'. This disposes some organisations to have nothing to do with them.

Figure 8

OPTIONS FOR WORKING WITH BUSINESS SCHOOLS

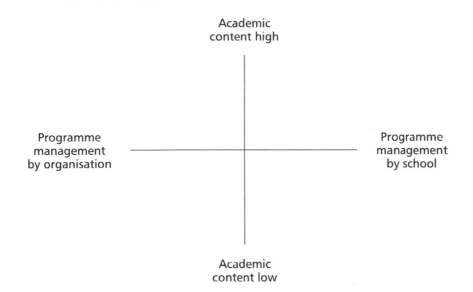

We have choices based on Figure 8. We can outsource entirely to a school or, at the other extreme, invite occasional speakers to address events managed by us.

What added value can a school bring? It is rich in learning resources and can provide an ambiance of innovation, exploration and discussion that may not be possible in other premises. It provides opportunities for networking that can have a special quality when combined with that ambiance.

Learning partnerships

A partnership implies an alliance with gains from the kind of customer–supplier relationship that may be merely contractual. In other cultures, trusting relationships are the essence of business, and these are not built on single transactions.

Figure 9 shows a map of different kinds of learning partnerships. Mutual advantage can be gained from planned learning between an organisation and several others with whom it is associated.

Figure 9

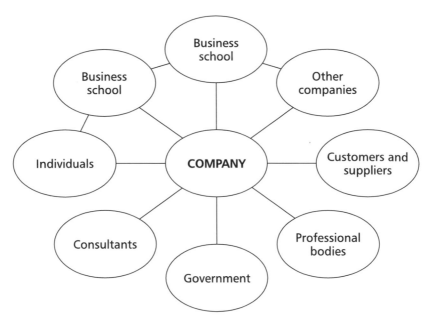

ORGANISATIONAL LEARNING PARTNERSHIPS

A growing area here is 'shared learning' between supplier and customer – that is, studying together the overall market that they share or building relationships together. This can extend to the mutual secondment of staff. Such exchanges have often proved of great value between organisations and government departments. The business school relationship can be developed so that individual faculty members extend into consultancy and coaching; internships can be offered; and a school can become a partner in the management of change. As the diagram shows, such a relationship can be extended to involve one or more other schools, or, through learning 'consortiums', other companies also.

Should any of HRD be outsourced?

Some organisations today have a general policy that they do not want to invest management time and effort in anything that is not their core business. Every kind of specialist service provider has arisen as a result. The management of the service is given totally to the provider and monitored against strict performance criteria. Experience of the success of such services is very mixed. What are the arguments on each side in respect of the HRD department?

For	*Against*
■ Reduced direct overhead cost	■ Lack of commitment to organisational goals
■ Reduced management attention	■ Lack of long-term ownership
■ Ability to control against strict performance criteria	■ Degrees of freedom in controlling performance
■ Availability of wider range of skills	■ Risks in lack of continuity of key skills

The strategic decision will be much affected by the general organisational approach to the importance of HRD. If HRD is seen as a vital strategic support to business goals, the management at least of HRD needs to be firmly in-house. However, there are operational activities that may well be outsourced – the management of facilities, the creation of materials and certain categories of regular training.

The use of consultants

The HRDM may be subject to general organisational policies regarding the use of consultants; indeed, some organisations exclude them in principle. Others have stringent guidelines for their use, including levels of spend, 'accreditation', references, contractual terms, or being on approved lists. The HRD area attracts more than most the independent practitioner with his or her niche of expertise and client relations. There is therefore plenty of choice. Long-term relationships can be built, and consultants can share in the organisation development process and seriously absorb the culture. Areas of consultant help include:

▐ assistance with determining the strategic HRD framework: sometimes consultants can see an overview or collate views given to them from different sources which add a new perspective to that held by the HRDM

▐ working with top management to establish their considered approach to people development

▐ researching learning needs and client perceptions

▐ setting up learning partnerships

▐ designing, running and evaluating specific programmes

▐ designing and implementing systems and processes

▐ the evaluation of resourcing choices

▐ programme/event evaluation

▐ benchmarking with other organisations

▐ facilitating 'political' workshops or meetings

▐ presenting particular messages at corporate events.

The choice of consultants is sometimes a nightmare for HRD owing to the plethora of large, medium and individual resources available. Ex-staff are frequently used, or those with whom long-standing relationships exist. Trying out new resources is a risk because there is rarely the opportunity for 'piloting'. Lists of clients in consultant's publicity may look impressive but go back years. It is therefore important to get focused references –

not just on the company but on the individuals themselves with whom you might be working, and to be satisfied that they will provide the right chemistry with the target audience.

> Study how consultants are being used in HRD activities across your organisation. Are there some consistent patterns? Taken as a whole, does it represent a sensible use of internal and external resources, given the talent available internally? Could there be other opportunities where consultants might add value?

In brief

- Thorough needs analysis that is business-driven will almost always yield more demand than can be met. A system of prioritisation is essential. We need to use systematic cost-benefit analysis but will always have to balance it with political considerations.

- Sometimes resourcing decisions are made for HRD, especially when it comes to premises and budgets. However, the more knowledgeable and prepared the HRDM is about the best use of resources, the greater will be his or her ability to convince others of what he or she believes is right for the organisation. Never be caught by surprise!

- When it comes to having a training centre, there are other considerations than cost. Would we benefit from a place that consolidates a desired culture?

- Networking is a key activity for HRD – internally and externally. Not only should HRD have its own network, but it is a key part of its role to ensure that a 'network of networks' exists across organisational boundaries.

- We looked at different strategies for internal funding and pricing. The choice is strategic, because it will give potent messages to the organisation.

■ A vital decision for the HRDM is how to co-ordinate the different contributions to people development. This will lead to defining roles and a capability framework that will support it.

■ Choosing between internal and external resources should be primarily driven by the added value of internal staff, which should be utilised to the maximum. It is very easy to be diverted into activities that someone else external could do.

■ HRD should explore the potential of different kinds of learning partnerships, and be sure to use consultants effectively as a complement to internal resources.

7

Marketing and Political Considerations

HRD is a supporting function and inevitably takes second place to business operational priorities. To be proactive and influential requires competing for attention, and therefore political and influencing skills. It can of course just get on with its activities relatively undisturbed – until the next review of overheads prompts the question whether it is adding any value. It can be caught out if not regularly assessing its success on this and other parameters.

All organisations have their political maps, rather like snakes-and-ladders boards. Altruistic employees who deplore politics in organisations are merely ignorant of the ways in which people work together – people with potentially competing objectives, overlapping accountabilities, individual power and influence aspirations, and genuine passions about the way things should be done. Politics can be divided into the 'natural' – defined by Rosemary Harrison as 'the art of achieving the possible' – and into 'powerplay', where the aims of an individual or group may not be synchronised with the goals of the organisation. It is often believed, for example by business school professors, that organisations continuously *seek* rational models for their decisions and behaviours. They may well value these, but other factors muddy their actions and decisions. *Homo organisationalis* is complex and all too human.

We have to remind ourselves of course that HRD has no given right to exist as a function except in so far as it does add value to the organisation. As we have seen in this book, this should not be difficult. But just as HRD sits in a political sea, it may well have an agenda of its own, for example:

■ survival
■ growth
■ higher status
■ influencing acceptance of its own values or interests
■ new or different facilities
■ wanting or not wanting to be outsourced
■ external revenue generation
■ public recognition through external conferences and publications.

This book is focused on how to do the right things for the *organisation*, and we shall proceed on the basis that the HRDM has the greater interests of the organisation at heart and look at some of the issues that influence his or her effectiveness.

There is always a shadow side to organisations

Uncomfortable as it is for many, there is always a 'shadow' side to organisations, despite all the grand visions and values and promises that are written down and published or formally discussed in meetings. Late-night bar discussions usually surface it all! In daily life, this substantially influences productivity, stress levels, motivation and commitment, and the quality of life.

One of the many failures of traditional accountancy is that it cannot distinguish between costs that contribute to value and those that do not. The 'negative' expenditures of time, travel costs, equipment, etc, are all lumped together with those that positively contribute to value for stakeholders. So many of the effects of the 'shadow side' are invisible to numbers-oriented management. It is a recommended strategy for HRD to make estimates from time to time of some of these hidden costs – for example, the loss of productivity from poor leadership, the cost of duplication due to lack of knowledge-sharing, or the cost of resolving a customer problem that should not have happened if the right capability had been in place.

Guiding Principle 21

In business, and even in most public-sector organisations today, numbers speak louder than words.

Politics in organisations is about steering through this shadow side, and includes such obstacles as:

■ *organisational walls* – Structures create boundaries, which condition the behaviour of people. Previously co-operating, they can start competing as shared objectives give way to rival ones. Communication becomes strained across the boundaries, and people focus inwards within their organisational space.

■ *business and organisational gaps* – These are like white space on an organisation chart, where accountabilities are owned by no one and it is impossible to grasp a lever for change.

■ *idiosyncrasies and personal agendas of individuals* – Inevitably people use organisations to satisfy their own drivers and ambitions, and these may not be at all synergistic with the organisation's strategies. (Some organisational cultures are more powerful than any individual, but they are few.)

■ *national and local cultures and traditions* – The way things are done 'here' is and always will be different.

The effect of any of these may be to work against the logical systematic approach that we have taken in following our model.

Top management support is vital

In order to be aligned with the business at all, some level of top management support and interest is essential. It is usually the case that the CEO, or equivalent, sets patterns that others follow, and his or her priorities and values are closely observed. Table 24 shows some of the considerations relating to different levels of support.

Table 24

LEVELS OF MANAGEMENT SUPPORT

Type of support	Characteristics	HRD response
CEO drives HRD agenda personally	HRD involved in major strategic decisions Priorities set by CEO Constant review by CEO	Close contact with business issues Flexibility of resources Strong influencing skills
Top team full commitment	Regular briefings/dialogues take place Priorities debated and agreed Focus on return	Uses top team commitment as backer of messages Involves directors in appropriate programmes
Individual director sponsorship	Driving force behind sponsored programmes	Exploits business advantages of sponsorship and seeks to extend
Subcommittee of board as 'steering group'	Likely that HRDM is secretary Reviews programmes and suggests advice on priorities	'Manages' the committee Uses decisions effectively
Passive CEO support	Signs documents relating to HRD on request Shows support when asked	Utilises willingness to give desired messages Seeks greater interest
HR director as champion	HR represents views of HRD and board	Thorough briefing Close familiarity with HRD
No representation	Control by budgets	Seeks better representation

To some extent this is a hierarchy of desirability. The chief executive who has a personal conviction of the vital support that HRD can give to the organisation is of course a great asset, even if he or she makes life uncomfortable for the HRDM. If it is only shared superficially by other senior players, it can be dangerous, because a widespread base of support is needed. Co-operation because it is 'politically correct' to do so may be only half-hearted. So the second level in the Table is highly desirable, and gives the HRDM regular access to dialogue with the team as well as endorsement of priorities.

Specific sponsorship for sections of HRD activity is also valuable for maintaining close business links. Thus the marketing director may sponsor all programmes connected with the development of sales and marketing people. It is often the case that cultural change or, for example, leadership initiatives, will be sponsored by the HR director. There are advantages in an operational director driving them, however.

> Which levels of support do you enjoy at the moment? Which would you like to have? Do other support functions have more interest taken in them? If so, analyse the support they have and see why it is. Are there some lessons to be learned? Talk to some HRDMs in other companies and assess their level of support. Is there anything to learn from how they have achieved what they have? Put together a plan for increasing the level of support from senior management.

Sometimes we have to challenge what top management think they want

Top management not only seeks to decide the direction of an organisation but may also prescribe in some detail the routes to achievement. Its view of change and of people development is more often than not coloured by its own personal values and motivations, and it sometimes needs to be guided into the perspectives of people lower down. The tendency to go for the 'blanket' solution is an easy way to show action to shareholders, parent companies or employees. A classic case is the response to poor customer-satisfaction results – where the knee-jerk reaction may be to put everyone through a 'customer care programme'. It may well be the case that the front-line people are the last who need this – the cause of the dissatisfaction lies in lack of resources, inefficient logistics, a lack of management visibility, or any of a host of other reasons.

Copying what other organisations do is also prevalent, and may be encouraged by consultants. However, if the 'eight-step' methodology can be followed rigorously, at least HRD has some ground for challenge.

Analysing the level of involvement that we have in strategic decision areas

In Table 1 (page 9) we outlined some areas of involvement with business strategy. Table 25 looks at the involvement of HRD specifically in the business drivers that we described in Chapter 3. There are three levels of involvement suggested:

■ *defining* – part of the group that decides on the outcome

■ *consulting* – providing specialist advice to, or perhaps facilitating, the group in its decision-making

■ *implementing* – making the decision a reality.

This book would argue that there should be a 'D' in every column on 'Implementing'. HRDMs need to decide the extent to which, if they 'backwards integrated', they believe it would be helpful for their organisation and HRD. Extensive involvement for its *own* sake may increase the standing of the HRDM but may be very time-consuming.

Table 25

STRATEGIC PARTNERSHIP – LEVELS OF INVOLVEMENT

Business link	Defining A D	Consulting A D	Implementing A D	Examples
Mission/vision				
Values				
Beliefs on people development				
Defining core capabilities				
Business strategies				
Business goals and plans				
Change programmes				
Organisational change plans				
Manpower plans				
External/ environmental changes				
Individual manager/ team goals				
Operational problems				
Team and individual learning needs				

(Tick 'A' for 'actual' and 'D' for 'desired')

The last column (Examples) refers to the ways in which involvement takes place. This might include some or all of:

- membership of strategic planning committees
- membership of performance improvement teams

∎ membership of quality circles

∎ membership of change management teams

∎ membership of new product introduction teams

∎ attendance at operational business reviews

∎ facilitating strategic workshops for business teams

∎ one-to-one dialogues with managers

∎ focus groups with cross-boundary groups

∎ systematic training-needs analysis

∎ leading or belonging to task forces and special project teams

∎ performance appraisal consultancy.

> Do this exercise for the part of the organisation for which you are responsible. Don't overstress the 'D' elements – choose it where you really feel HRD's involvement would make a difference. What mechanisms could you use to close the gaps between 'A' and 'D'? Who might be able to help you do that?

How can HRD gain more support and influence?

As in all relationships, finding a bridge to what someone cares about or believes in themselves is what gives us an entry-point. How can the HRDM change perceptions and exert influence? The answer is by:

∎ finding out, first and foremost, what interests and preoccupies the 'target' – showing a prime concern for supporting his/her/their objectives and agendas

∎ demonstrating an understanding of the business or operations; what the key measures are and what challenges/problems are being experienced

∎ making formal connections into business decisions through membership of project teams, review bodies and steering groups

■ demonstrating real bottom-line and organisational effectiveness gains from well-managed training interventions

■ publicising success stories internally, especially those that affect business results

■ gaining good publicity for the organisation through the media and public platforms

■ creating strong links with people who influence the organisation as a whole and creating added value for them

■ sound benchmarking with competitors or leading organisations, and questioning the positioning of his or her own organisation against them. (A good question for top management is 'If competitors are investing more than we are in developing their people, what implications does this have?')

The personal credibility of the HRDM

This will be a powerful door to opportunities and influence. It is not just a question of being viewed positively by colleagues in the various parts of the organisation – unfortunately, there are risks of 'negative credibility' also, and image is a notoriously fickle creature.

Below is a suggested 'balance sheet' of *personal* credibility. (It inevitably reflects the author's personal experience, and that is limited to the organisations he has worked with and the lessons he has himself had to learn.)

Table 26

THE BALANCE SHEET OF CREDIBILITY

Assets	Liabilities
Business knowledge and experience	No experience other than HR or HRD
Business understanding	Expert knowledge in guru-speak
Listening to business problems with interest	Talking psycho-babble and seeing every problem as having a soft-centred solution
Logical argument	Emotional argument
Accepting reality	Refusing to accept the shadow side of organisations
Working with reality	Working with dreams and idealism, living in hope of Utopia
Respect for all	Respect only for perceived role models
Personal charisma	Skewed personality
Caring passionately about people development, rejoicing in their success	HRD is just a job to be done
Self-aware; conscious of others' perceptions	Unaware of impact of own behaviour
Social skills	Unwilling to socialise
Persuasive skills	Dogmatic style
Problem-centred consultancy	Solution-centred prescription
Helping people learn from each other	Wanting to control learning
Natural sharer and collaborator	Internally focused, jealous of personal knowledge
Taking time to network, internally/externally	Lost in a personal world
Understanding the need for short-term gains	Expecting people to buy into the long term naturally

(continued opposite)

Table 26 (*continued*)

THE BALANCE SHEET OF CREDIBILITY

Assets	Liabilities
Looking for opportunities to help and support	Looking for opportunities to push own agenda
Looking for allies and working with them	Coming in tangentially
Able to manage the 'shadow side'	Regarding politics as irrelevant
Money-conscious	Regarding money as a nuisance factor
Data-oriented	Dealing in immeasurables
Taking time to get to know people personally	Working through paper and e-mail
Brave in standing up for values and beliefs	Blowing with the wind
Doing what he or she promises	Enjoying talking rather than doing
Talking about success in manager's language	Talking about success in HRD language
Flexibility and adaptability	Perfection

This is a somewhat unstructured 'capability' profile of an HRDM. Not all items have the same weight, and much depends on the political and cultural environment as to what would be regarded as desirable.

Ask some line managers what they would add, modify or delete in Table 26. Then ask some people you feel it important to influence how they would score you on each line from 1 to 10. (This could be done on an anonymous 360-degree format, if desired.) What lessons for your own development can be drawn?

Guiding Principle 22

Maturity in a support function is learning to work with and from reality, rather than wishing it was not there.

Marketing and publicity

Marketing HRD as a whole

Internal marketing sometimes seems to absorb more creativity and effort than are focused on real customers. Nevertheless, it has to be done, and it follows the same rules as any other kind of marketing. It is to do with image and reputation (perceptions), and with clarity of communication as to its purpose and ability to help. It requires:

- ▍ a memorable and sensitive 'branding' that gives the right message yet is sensitive to any potential negative reactions (ICL Learning gave itself the strapline *Systems Integrators in Learning*, which reflected the business strapline of the time)

- ▍ the 'liftspeech' that describes succinctly what HRD's role is

- ▍ using language that people easily relate to (avoiding HR jargon)

- ▍ understanding who potential customers are and clearly communicating messages to them that generate interest for them

- ▍ developing continuing relationships with key influencers

- ▍ making it easy for customers to find out how HRD helps and what it offers (quality documentation, web pages)

- making it easy for customers to do business with HRD (help-desks, e-mail, html links)
- monitoring feedback and satisfaction with events and services regularly
- responding to complaints and difficulties promptly.

History is always with us. Training may have had low status and been populated by ex-operational managers deemed to have failed at their jobs or been 'put out to grass'. They may have established themselves as course providers and not been seen to have any strategic impact at all. Organisationally, they may be seen as tucked away in a cul-de-sac. So credibility may have to be built through a steady plan of discussion and publicity. The HRDM would look for opportunities to:

- make presentations to the top management committee
- make presentations to business unit team meetings
- take part in corporate conferences
- exploit intranets, web pages and other corporate communication media
- feature HRD staff and their achievements
- go in for any departmental competitions, corporate prizes, etc.

> What methods of communication and publicity are you using today? How are they perceived by the people you are trying to help? (Ask a few informally.) What could you do more effectively? What could you add to your current range?

One part of a learning partnership may be to offer expertise and help in HRD to real customers of the business. Without necessarily selling any services to them, a seminar or discussion group can be set up that shares HRD's thinking and programmes. Business managers will appreciate this support and talk about it to others, if it is done well.

Another is to offer a prize, for example, for 'excellence in learning initiatives'. People can be nominated, a jury set up, and winners announced with suitable fanfares. Not only can good learning ideas be promoted, but so also can the role of HRD in encouraging learning wherever it happens.

Telling people what we plan to do

We may well have put together a strategy with key directions and prioritised activities that are absolutely business-driven and designed in every way to support business achievement. That does not mean that everyone will automatically play his or her part.

Guiding principle 23

When it comes to releasing time and money, there are a host of things that are 'good candidates', and every manager has to make choices. Never assume that your case is unassailable.

Once again, we need influencing skills, and the secret as always is to understand the needs and values of the person or people we are talking to. Logic and business needs are not enough, important as they are. One may well get acceptance of an idea, but no real support because there is no answer to the famous WIIFM question: 'What's In It For Me?' The greater good of the organisation as a whole or longer-term benefits may strike no chords in someone who expects to move on in a couple of years, or for whom current local success is absolutely predominant in his or her thinking.

So we have a spectrum of 'partnership':

Passive acceptance	Agreed support	Total commitment
'Seems like a good idea'	'Count on me to play my part when necessary'	'Please get me and my people actively involved'

Achieving the left-hand end of the scale is not difficult. After all, HRD deals in 'making things better, improving performance, developing people' – few will dispute the desirability of the offerings. But engaging hearts as well as brains, and then feet and hands, is a sales process. Selling is about helping people to clarify their need, and then showing how that need can be met. This is the essence of the learning consultant's core skill.

> Create a 'map' of support in the organisation – take top managers, other HR professionals, key line managers, and other support functions. Use as axes 'Strategic importance for HRD' and 'Strength of support'. What are the factors that contribute to the different positionings? How could you strengthen support where needed?

When it comes to *information* we need to follow all the rules of marketing – helping the right people to know the right things at the right time. This may require a series of communications covering different groups of people.

Telling the organisation the good things we have done

Successful programme delivery is our best publicity. Making the strategy happen gives HRD a real chance to demonstrate its ability to contribute to business and personal success.

Business is no different from life: we like to back winners. Demonstrating the success of a strategy and its resultant initiatives is critical for preparing the ground for future strategies. Perhaps the initial strategy in a particular year was scaled down or not given the budget it required for implementation. Demonstrating success allows a second opportunity at a later date to revisit old ideas, or to introduce more daring ideas, or simply to gain support for the department.

Publicising success stories is a powerful form of marketing. Again, internal media can be used – but also external. Speaking at conferences and seminars, or writing articles for such magazines as *People Management*, *Industrial and Commercial Training*, *Organisation and People* and others gives publicity both internally and externally, especially if the company runs a 'cuttings service' for senior managers.

Winning awards is yet another form of powerful publicity. Although a lot of work may be involved – and that has to be seriously evaluated – achieving National Training Awards (NTAs) or industry-based special awards can be used to great effect. The achievement of Investors In People (IIP) status is perhaps the most useful award to have for external purposes, and has its own spin-off in attracting staff and enhancing corporate image.

> What does HRD's 'cuttings book' look like for the last two years? List any opportunities for telling the world good things you have done.

How should HRD be positioned in the organisation?

Over the years, personnel and training and development have become more and more closely associated, although it was not always thus. Now we talk of HR and HRD, the latter almost defined as a subset of the former. (Personally I could argue for this to be reversed! One of the most innovative HR organisations in the UK –

Birmingham Midshires Building Society – has in its management team a 'head of people development' as the most senior HR representative.) Organisations are still very functionally driven, each with their own territories to protect, and an enormous amount of non-value-added effort is expended in issues to do with these territories. There is a strong argument to think away from the traditional box about support activities – some are administrative, some are control-driven, others are to do with achieving better performance. HRD is essentially about *change* and performance improvement.

In non-hierarchical organisations, HRD would be a self-standing team that provides a service to other teams. (Indeed, one area of influence HRD can have is in the encouragement of new organisational models.) However, such are rare. In some hierarchies and bureaucracies, status signals such as grade and title can affect the ability to influence or be listened to. This should not be a blocker in our thinking – doing the right things, and doing them well with credible contributors, can override organisation charts.

The physical positioning of HRD can give a message. If *all* are located in the corporate 'training centre' – or equivalent – it is distanced from the daily operations, and people perceive it as a peripheral service. So some creativity and sacrifice of 'managerial convenience' may help to show integration with the business.

As we noted on page 162, it is probably a mistake to confuse internal HRD with external training revenue businesses. The goals, motivations and skills needed by the one are quite different from those needed by the other.

It may be advantageous to appoint an 'HRD steering committee' made up of key managers and led by a particular champion of people development. This provides a platform not only for guidance but for exploration of ideas and sharing of thoughts on priorities.

Corporate 'universities'

Particularly in the USA, there has been a growth in so-called corporate universities. (A famous UK example is Unipart in Oxford.) The European Foundation of Management Development held a seminar in 1997 to study these, and it appeared that many were 'previous training departments with delusions of grandeur'. It is a fashionable term to use for a centralised training and education establishment. An alternate name is the 'corporate learning centre' – which seems a contradiction in terms if one believes that most learning comes from the workplace. One of the best known – that of General Electric – is just called GE Crotonville, but is seen very firmly as a central developer of values and culture. Some have been set up as in-house versions of business schools whereas others operate 'virtually', using electronic distribution of learning material. One interesting variation is 'Aquae Universitas', or the University of Water, set up by Anglian Water. This is nothing to do with training at all but is a systematic repository of company knowledge. Senior managers take ownership for 'faculties' who look after the use and growth of knowledge and experience in a designated area.

There is a sense of grandeur about the corporate university that may appeal to some CEOs a lot more than to the employees. We need to remember:

Guiding Principle 24

We should not follow fashions but look for a positioning that will reinforce the key messages that we want to give about people development.

The prestige of management education

Association with a prestigious business or management school may be very seductive. Many an HRDM has been tasked with the job of assessing 'what is available' in order to choose an appropriate partner. The criteria for selection may not be totally based on maximising learning for the organisation. As far as possible, the HRDM should maintain this as his or her priority – because a lot of money will be involved and all such investments are eventually called to account.

There may be conflicting messages between HR and HRD

Regardless of reporting relationships, it is often the case that HR and HRD are very busy in their own right pursuing their separate goals and may not be well co-ordinated. HRD is frequently associated in managers' minds with HR, and this can be a problem to both sides, depending on their respective credibility. The greatest danger is that of mixed messages. Examples of where some confusion may arise are shown in Table 27:

Table 27

POSSIBLE DIFFERENCES BETWEEN HR AND HRD MESSAGES

HRD approach	HR approach
Career development is about continuous personal growth	Progress is visible through going up the grading system
Personal ownership of careers and development is ideal	Job descriptions emphasise managerial control of development
We need people with a flexible and adaptable mindset	We must have consistency of terms, conditions and benefits
We must reward people for the value they bring to the organisation	We must pay people according to the value of their job
We should see job vacancies as learning opportunities	We should fill each job with the best candidate available

(continued on page 194)

Table 27 (continued)

POSSIBLE DIFFERENCES BETWEEN HR AND HRD MESSAGES

HRD approach	HR approach
The appraisal system is primarily about development	The appraisal system is primarily about performance management
We should always try to retain people who are valuable assets	We cannot afford what is not in the headcount plan

The one side represents a view of organisations as concerned with maximising and valuing individual growth; the other is about hierarchical systems of consistency and control into which individuals are fitted. Hopefully, these dichotomies do not exist, but it is quite likely that the two sides are moving at different paces. Individuals may embrace the mindset of the left only to find that the right is not yet ready to reinforce it.

Although it could be said to be firmly in the court of the HR director to avoid these confusions, the HRDM will want to assist in the co-ordination of messages.

Final thought

We have observed before that because many HR and HRD practitioners think that what they are doing is leading-edge practice, *and* they can show a logical link to business benefit, they believe that key business managers should welcome their efforts with open arms.

In my first HR role reporting to a managing director, Tony, I followed the due process of the time and asked him to set my objectives for the year. He thought for a minute and then said, 'Andrew, I wouldn't have selected you if I felt you could not determine what needed to be done professionally yourself. I shall judge you on the basis of whether your colleagues on the management team find you helpful in the achievement of *their* business goals.' I was often conscious of the desire to do so-called 'leading-edge' projects, and – it must be said – gave in to that desire from time to time, but Tony's simple message is one that I have never forgotten.

In brief

- HRD cannot escape from being in the political arena. To be strategic means to be involved in all parts and at all levels in the organisation. HRD has to learn how to cope with 'the shadow side' of organisations and when it is appropriate to influence and seek change.

- It needs to evaluate where its support resides, and who its champions are. It may need to create some more of these and extend its reach of support. This can be done by many means, all involving effort and dialogue.

- In addition, HRD should evaluate its actual and desirable involvement in the strategic drivers, and assess whether this should be extended.

- Credibility of any support function is the key to influence. HRD needs feedback as to how it is perceived, as does the HRDM personally, and this should be actively sought.

- Internal marketing is essential – of the function and its role, of its activities, and of its successes. Good publicity is powerful marketing in its own right.

- Setting up 'HRD steering groups' of respected people in the organisation can be a powerful source of influence as well as guidance.

- We need to beware of conflicts in approach and message between HR and HRD, and do our best to ensure that they are resolved.

- At the end of the day, will managers say we *helped* them – as individuals, yes – but also in their business achievements?

A Appendix

Hertfordshire
COUNTY COUNCIL

CORPORATE
TRAINING & DEVELOPMENT
STRATEGY

The development of all our staff is central to the achievement of the Council's strategic intent.

We will support people so that they welcome and can cope with the changes which we need to make. This will underpin all development activities.

Success will only be achieved by releasing and realising the potential of the people we employ.

CONTEXT

Change continues to accelerate and pressures on the Council's resources grow. This has a direct impact on our employees and it is this framework of change and supporting our staff to meet it which sets the agenda for training and development. Issues include the ongoing moves towards a more commercial approach. Market testing and White Collar CCT will in the short and medium term be a particular feature of this. The key driver of change will however be the work which is currently in progress to develop the County Agenda with emphasis on cross-functional and inter-agency working and locally based service delivery.

These changes will affect the ways in which people work and are managed bringing:

- further decentralisation and devolution
- flatter management structures and a slimmer and leaner organisation
- stress on measurable performance and quality initiatives
- continued emphasis on competence
- need for a flexible work force
- fewer specialists directly employed
- project based and cross functional working
- empowered rather than command structures
- partnership approach to service delivery/suppliers/employees

This will bring a need for an enhanced and in some cases an entirely new skill base which we will support our staff to develop.

STRATEGIC ISSUES

Working within this context five key issues emerge:

1. HOW TO CREATE A DEVELOPMENT AND LEARNING CULTURE WITHIN THE COUNCIL

   Training and development must be placed on the Council's strategic agenda and commitment to staff development needs to be identified as a key corporate value.

2. HOW TO DEVELOP MANAGERS FOR THE FUTURE

Identifying the competencies which will define managerial success and creating development solutions to build them.

3. HOW TO RESPOND TO THE COUNTY AGENDA

Supporting corporate initiatives and addressing the emerging development needs of all groups of staff as new demands are placed upon them.

4. HOW TO DEVELOP STAFF TO MEET THE DEMANDS OF COMPETITION

With White Collar CCT on the agenda the need to provide development for staff in both the client and provider roles will have a renewed emphasis.

5. HOW TO RESPOND TO THE NATIONAL TARGETS FOR EDUCATION AND TRAINING AND TO NATIONAL VOCATIONAL QUALIFICATIONS

As National Vocational Qualifications (NVQs) become embedded and available for all occupational groups a corporate response becomes increasingly important.

PURSUING OUR STRATEGY

We are committed to the following actions to pursue our strategy:

CREATING A DEVELOPMENT AND LEARNING CULTURE

- A Staff Development Charter will be introduced
- The manager's role as a developer of staff will be developed
- Investors in People will be used to improve staff development processes
- Targets will be set for achieving IIP/Performance Management/Personal Development Plans
- The relevance of training will be demonstrated through improved identification of training needs and evaluation
- The training and development implications of all strategic issues will be considered
- Mechanisms will be established to ensure that members, chief officers and senior managers shape and approve the corporate training programme
- Marketing of training and development opportunities will be improved to give them a higher profile

▎ Improved mechanisms to improve resourcing will be introduced

DEVELOPING MANAGERS FOR THE FUTURE

▎ Management competencies will be defined

▎ The SPACE programme will be refocused in line with these competencies and calls for a qualification based management programme

▎ A wider development programme will be introduced for people who have completed SPACE so that they can continue their development

▎ Management development will be fitted into the wider context of the human resource strategies needed to take us into the next millennium

RESPONDING TO THE COUNTY AGENDA

▎ Programmes to help staff understand and cope with the process of change will continue to be made available

▎ Managers will be developed as influencers of change

▎ Project management training will be introduced

▎ There will be involvement in the strategic planning process to ensure that development issues are on the agenda

▎ Resources will be available to support new corporate initiatives as they emerge

DEVELOPING STAFF TO MEET THE DEMANDS OF COMMERCIALISM

▎ Training For Trading and for Client Managers will continue to be offered

▎ A programme of training for financial skills will also be introduced

RESPONDING TO THE NATIONAL TARGETS FOR EDUCATION AND TRAINING AND NVQS

▎ There will be a departmental approach to establish which of the targets should receive priority and to action this within local training strategies and plans

▎ NVQ related training for administrative support staff will be introduced

▎ NVQ related training for all 16-23 year olds will be encouraged

- The NVQ programme for supervisory development will continue to be offered
- Accreditation for our management, finance and client programmes will be pursued

DEVELOPMENT CHARTER

As an employee of the County Coouncil I will be working in an organisation in which learning is valued. I will be supported to undertake the training and development which I need to help me to achieve and maintain a high standard of performance and will be given the encouragement and support to achieve my full potential.

I AM ENTITLED TO:

- equality of opportunity in all aspects of my development
- an induction programme into my own job and department as well as the wider organisation
- an understanding of the direction and objectives of the Council and of my department
- an understanding of the contribution which is expected of me
- clear and measurable objectives for my performance at work
- an annual review of my performance
- a personal development plan which addresses my development needs. This will include on and off job development as well as personal learning.
- a manager who is committed to staff development

I WILL BE ENCOURAGED TO UNDERTAKE:

- continuous learning and development throughout my employment
- development to enhance my career prospects
- day release training to obtain the qualifications which I need to do my job
- planned work experience in a different department or organisation to broaden my skills and knowledge
- a planned and self-financing sabbatical where appropriate

I RECOGNISE THAT LEARNING IS A PERSONAL RESPONSIBILITY AND I WILL THEREFORE:

- share responsibility for identifying my development needs
- take advantage of development opportunities
- take an active part in performance management and staff development schemes
- take the initiative when I recognise opportunities for learning
- share my knowledge with others

Issued by the Personnel Department

A Message from the Chief Executive

This Development Charter is intended to give a very clear message about the high level of commitment we have to your personal development and the commitment we want you to have to your own learning.

It is only by developing our staff and equipping them with the skills and knowledge they need, that we will be able to meet the challenges of the agenda the Council has set itself to take us into the next millennium.

It is our aim to create a culture of learning and, to ensure that we make progress we are setting ourselves performance indicators and targets for training and development which will be monitored by both Chief Officers and County Councillors. We will also be evaluating the Development Charter and its impact and I look forward to hearing about the changes that you have been able to make.

Bill Ogley
Chief Executive.

FR Further Reading

BEE F. *and* BEE R. *Facilitation Skills*. London, Institute of Personnel and Development, 1998.

BOYDELL T. *and* LEARY M. *Identifying Training Needs*. London, Institute of Personnel and Development, 1996.

BRAMLEY P. *Evaluating Training*. London, Institute of Personnel and Development, 1996.

BURGOYNE J., PEDLER M. *and* BOYDELL T. *The Learning Company*. Maidenhead, McGraw-Hill, 1996.

CASTNER-LATTO J. (ed.) *Successful Training Strategies*. San Francisco, Calif., Jossey-Bass, 1988.

CONNOCK S. *HR Vision*. London, Institute of Personnel Management, 1991.

FITZ-ENZ J. *How to Measure Human Resource Management*. 2nd edn. Maidenhead, McGraw-Hill, 1995.

GOUGH J. *Developing Learning Materials*. London, Institute of Personnel and Development, 1996.

HACKETT P. *Introduction to Training*. London, Institute of Personnel and Development, 1997.

HARDINGHAM A. *Designing Training*. London, Institute of Personnel and Development, 1996.

HARDINGHAM A. *Psychology for Trainers*. London, Institute of Personnel and Development, 1998.

HARRISON R. *Employee Development*. London, Institute of Personnel and Development, 1997.

HONEY P. *and* MUMFORD A. *Managing in a Learning Environment*. Maidenhead, Peter Honey Publications, 1996.

KEARNS P. *and* MILLER T. *Measuring the Impact of Training and Development on the Bottom Line*. Hitchin, Technical Communications (Publishing) Ltd, 1996.

MABEY C. *and* SALAMAN G. *Strategic Human Resource Management*. London, Blackwell, 1996.

MAYO A. J. *Managing Careers: Strategies for organisations*. London, Institute of Personnel Management, 1992.

MAYO A. J. *and* LANK E. *The Power of Learning*. London, Institute of Personnel and Development, 1994.

MEGGINSON D. *and* WHITAKER V. *Cultivating Self-Development*. London, Institute of Personnel and Development, 1996.

MITCHELL A. Defining the Role of Corporate Learning Centres and Universities. *EFMD Forum*. Issue 97/3. October 1997.

PORRAS J. I. *and* COLLINS J. C. *Built to Last: Successful habits of visionary companies*. New York, Harpers Press, 1994.

REAY D. G. *Planning a Training Strategy*. London, Kogan Page, 1994.

SEMLER R. *Maverick*. London, Arrow, 1994.

SIDDONS S. *Delivering Training*. London, Institute of Personnel and Development, 1997.

SLOMAN M. *A Handbook for Training Strategy*. London, Gower, 1994.

Index